Boscobel: Or, the History of His Sacred Majesties ... Preservation After the Battle of Worcester [By T. Blount]. with a Suppl. to the Whole

Thomas Blount, Anne Wyndham

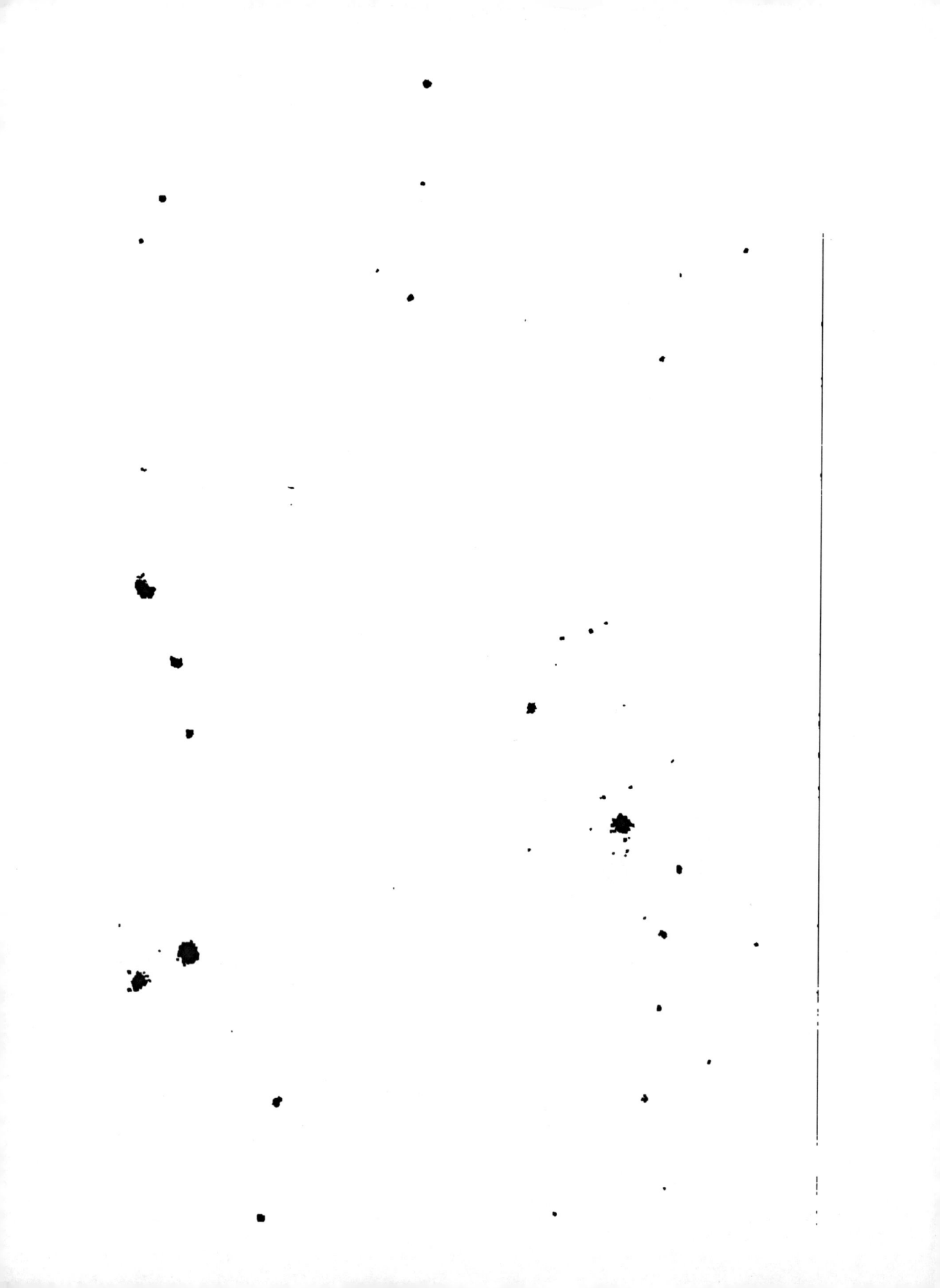

BOSCOBEL

BOSCOBEL:

OR, THE COMPLEAT

HISTORY

Of the Most Miraculous

PRESERVATION

OF

King *CHARLES* II.

After the BATTLE of *Worcester*:

APRIL the 3d, 1651.

To which is added,

Clauftrum Regale Referatum:

OR THE

King's CONCEALMENT at *Trent.*

Publifh'd by Mrs. ANN WYNDHAM.

The FIFTH EDITION.

With a SUPPLEMENT to the Whole.

LONDON:

Printed: And Sold by all Bookfellers, and Venders
of News and Subfcription-Books.

MDCCXLVIII.

TO ALL TRUE

LOYALISTS.

HE following Sheets were originally published in 1662, immediately after the Reftoration, when the Facts were frefh in Memory, and the Perfons concerned, perhaps, all living; which is a fufficient Proof of the Genuinenefs and Truth of the Account. The Credit of which ftands further undeniably confirmed by the Liberty the Author had of dedicating it to the Royal Sufferer Himfelf.

A 2 *THE*

THE noble Historian *and others, who have given us the History and Account of those Times,* are *too voluminous and expensive to be within the Reach of that Degree of Life, which will appear to have been the chief Instruments of preserving his Sacred Majesty;* they were not Persons *of great Families and Fortunes, who know that their* Honours *and* Estates *as they came from, so must* depend upon the Crown *(though I would by no Means lessen or depreciate the Merit of those* Noble Families *who engaged in the Royal Cause) but the* Loyal Man *of inferiour* Birth *and Fortune, unimproved by* Education *and* Learning, *who perhaps had never any other Knowledge of, or Acquaintance with the Name of* the King, *but the disagreeable one of paying* Taxes *to him: I say, when Men of this* low Rank *are not to be* deterred *by the utmost* Dangers, *not* corrupted *by the* largest Rewards, *not* influenced *by the* prevailing Principle *of* Interest; *in what a different* Light *does such* Virtue, *such* Loyalty *appear, from that of* the highest Rank, *whose certain Interest it is to be so. In Justice therefore to the Memory of those* faithful Persons, *who were the miraculous Instruments of the* King's Escape, *and*

and that their Names may be preserved from Oblivion, *and transmitted to the latest* Posterity, *with all the* Honour *due to them, the following History is restored to* Light. *It may teach the* Prince *to set a* true Value *upon the meanest of his* Subjects : *He sees when the* Lyon *is entangled, the lowest Animal may be of Service to him. It may teach the* People, *that though for the Sins of the Nation,* Anarchy *and* Confusion *is sometimes permitted to flourish, that* God *by whom* Kings reign, *does* miraculously preserve, *and in his own Time, as* miraculously *restore them. To see any human Creature in Distress, moves* Compassion *in a* generous Breast ; *but when* Royalty *is reduced to the last Extremity, even the Enemies to that Government can't but shed a Tear, if they are not harder than the* Adamant itself. *I own I cannot but tremble (though I own the happy Event) when I paint the* Bloody Regicides *under the* Royal Tree, *when I hear their* monstrous Imprecations *and* Curses *against* God *and his* Vicegerent ; *when I travel with that* unfortunate Prince *by the* Troops *of his* Enemies, *who* thirsted after his Blood, *and trace every wearisome and dangerous Step he took ; when I reflect upon the Secrecy that was preserved among such Numbers of all* Sorts and

Sexes,

Sexes, I *can think no more of any* Human Cause *or* Conduct, *but acknowledge the* divine Hand *in every Act, as visible as if the* Writing *had been upon the* Wall, *and must declare it the* Lord's Doings, *and* marvellous *in our Eyes.*

I chose to publish this at this Time, *in hopes that from the small* Expence *and* Shortness, *it may fall into the Hands of* Numbers, *who by seeing the* Miseries *brought on the* King *and* Kingdom *by the* unparrallel'd Wickedness *of those* Times, *they may for the future have a due Sense of the* Murder *of the* Thirtieth *of* January, *and treat the Act of that Day with* greater Abhorrence *and* Detestation *than the present Age seems to do; and may likewise celebrate annually the* Twenty-ninth *of* May, *with the same* Demonstrations *of* Joy, *as were shewn at the* Restoration.

THE

TO THE
READER.

Ehold, I present you with an History of Wonders; *Wonders so great, that, as no former Age can parallel, succeeding Times will* scarce believe them.

Expect here to read the highest Tyranny and Rebellion that was ever acted by Subjects, and the greatest Hardships and Persecutions that ever were suffer'd by a King; yet did His Patience exceed His Sorrows; and His Virtue became at last victorious.

Some Particulars, I confess, are so superlatively extraordinary, that I easily should fear they would scarce gain Belief, even from my modern Reader, had I not this strong Argument to secure me, that no ingenuous Person will think me so frontless, as knowingly to write an Untruth in an History where His Sacred Majesty (my dread Sovereign, and the best of Kings) bears the principal Part, and most of the other Persons concern'd in the same Action (except the Earl of Derby, Lord Wilmot and Colonel Blague) still alive, ready to pour out Shame and Confusion on so impudent a Forgery.

b   But

To the READER.

But I am so far from that foul Crime of publishing what's false, that I can safely say, I know not one Line unauthentick; such has been my Care, to be sure of the Truth, that I have dilligently collected the Particulars from most of their Mouths, who were the very Actors themselves in this Scene of Miracles.

To every individual Person (as far as my Industry could arrive to know) I have given the Due of his Merit; be it for Valour, Fidelity, or whatever other Quality that any Way had the Honour to relate to His Majesty's Service.

In this later Edition I have added some Particulars, which came to my Knowlege, since the Publication; and have observ'd, that in this Persecution, much of His Majesty's Actions and Sufferings have run parallel with those of King David.

And though the whole Complex may want Elegance and Politeness of Style (which the Nature of such Relations does not properly challenge) yet it cannot want Truth, the chief Ingredient for such Undertakings; in which Assurance I am not afraid to venture my self in your Hands.

Read on, and wonder.

The

To the READER.

The PLAIN-DEALER (*Numb.* 50, *which came out on* Friday Sept. *the* 11*th*, 1724.) *upon his reading* BOSCOBELL, *has the following* Words, *which were thought not improper to be prefix'd to the present Edition of this Book.*

" I There meet, *says he*, with such a pro-
"   digious Instance of Fidelity, and
" Loyalty, in a poor mean Country Fellow,
" nam'd *Penderell*, and all his *Family*, that
" I know not *any* so illustrious, to which my
" Heart would lead me to pay greater Ho-
" nour, or sincerer Acknowledgments of
" my Esteem. I am not at all surprized to
" find, that this amazing Incident of glo-
" rious Integrity, is cooly, and insensibly
" treated by Men of pretended but slender
" Abilities; who have an Affectation to
" shine upon more pompous Subjects; who
" chuse rather to spend their Vain Strength
" in relating the Fury, and the Fate, of
" that Battle, and lay out all that mistaken
" Eloquence in raising the Powers of Hell,
" and representing the Prince of Darkness,
" as lifting himself by Contract, under *Oli-*
" *ver*, and pushing on the criminal Succes-

To the READER.

" fes, and the horrible Triumphs, which
" he abtained. I am not in the leaft furpriz-
" ed at all this; but it is both a Matter of
" Surprize, and Confufion to think, that
" fo many truly great Poets and Orators,
" fhould live juft after, and leave an Ex-
" ample, fo beneficial to all Pofterity, to
" be in a Manner forgotten, for want of
" being commended, with that true Spi-
" rit and Warmth, which it fo richly de-
" ferves.

" PERHAPS, the Hiftory of the whole
" World were we to turn it never fo care-
" fully over, could furnifh us with but very
" few Things more furprizing, more a-
" ftonifhing, more moving and pathetick,
" more exemplary and edifying, than this
" too much neglected, this yet uncelebrated
" Paffage! — A Monarch to be forc'd, by
" a prevailing Faction, to turn a Fugitive,
" in his own Kingdoms, to fave his Life!
" And when difcomfitted Princes, difabled
" Lords, and routed Armies could not any
" longer affift their Sovereign, that it fhould
" be referved by Providence, for a poor
" fimple Hind to preferve this Lord's A-
" nointed from a cruel purfuing Victor,
" whofe vaft and præternatural Swells of
" Fortune made him foon grow the Dread
" and

" and Terror of all *Chriſtendom!* — That
" it ſhould be reſerved for a poor igno-
" rant Countryman, to ſave a wiſe and
" mighty Prince from falling, like his good
" Father, to move our Pity, who was after-
" wards, by the Means of this wonderful
" Preſervation, received as our Glory, with
" the Applauſes and Acclamations, not
" only of our own three Kingdoms, but
" almoſt all the neighbouring Nations
" round about us! And ſhall this *Engliſh-*
" *man* be left to be recorded with Honour
" by foreign Writers, and be only coldly
" ſpoken of by our own? — Is he a mean
" Man? Conſider the noble Truſt, and the
" noble Diſcharge of it! and he grows
" great in Honour, in Proportion to the
" Meanneſs of his Condition. Is he poor!
" How does that Poverty add to the Rich-
" neſs of his Virtue, who hears *Præmium*
" bid for the precious Life, he has in
" Cuſtody, and yet, diſdaining the Bribe
" of Gold, would rather venture his own
" Life for his Loyalty, than get a Liveli-
" hood by turning a Traytor? Sure, no-
" thing but a narrow minded Soul, which
" is abandon'd to a Spirit of Barbarity and
" Meanneſs, can let a little Idea of him
" enter his Thoughts, upon the Account

b 3   " of

To the R E A D E R.

" of his being a mean and defpicable Fi-
" gure. It is the nobleft Addition to his
" Greatnefs! As inconfiderable as he might
" be otherwife, he muft in this View, make
" a fine Picture in the Imagination of all
" Men of Honour; and he is a living Dif-
" grace to all thofe titled Criminals, who
" followed the gay, but wicked Fortunes,
" and partook in the Impious Greatnefs, of
" the Purfuer of Majefty. Thofe only,
" who look no farther than the outfide of
" Things, will think him, becaufe a *Ple-*
" *bian,* below *Eulogy*; but I, who view
" him with the fame Eyes as the *Romans*
" would a Dictator at his Plough, almoft
" think him above it. Had he liv'd in the
" Times of the *Latin* Bards, and been the
" Preferver of an *Auguftus*, his honeft Con-
" tempt of bribing Gold, would have juft-
" ly given him a Place equal with *Camillus,*
" in the famous *Horation* Ode, confecrated
" to the Praifes of that Emperor.

" IT is to me a Scene, that the Imagi-
" nation cannot entertain without a Mix-
" ture of Grief and Admiration, when we
" feem to place before our Eyes that Prince
" difguifed in the Habit of a Ruftick, and
" going thro' fo many Different Dangers,
" relying upon the Conduct and Fidelity

of

To the R E A D E R.

" of this *real* Ruftick, this venerable Clown,
" and his little Family, for his Guards. I
" remember to have heard a great many
" fay, That, *tho' he has heard the King tell*
" *the Story in jeft, he has wondered to fee many*
" *fmile, when his Majefty faid pleafantly, That,*
" He was once in Danger of lofing his
" Guide, in the Night-time, but that the
" ruffling of *Richard's* Calves-Skin Breeches
" was a Direction to his Ear in the Dark.
" *The King might, indeed, make a Jeft of it*
" *himfelf, faid he, but I could find no Room*
" *for thinking of Majefty in fuch Diftrefs,*
" *without being forrowful in earneft, with a*
" *Grief, which was beyond the Notion of an*
" *odd and comical Drefs to remove."* ——— I
" muft fay the fame, as this Nobleman,
" with regard to the King; and when I
" confider *Penderell* on the other Hand,
" there is fomething too ferious in his Inte-
" grity, not to make us lofe all Thoughts
" of his Appearance, and venerate him in
" the Habit of a Clown. As there was a
" princely Perfon in one rough Garb; fo
" was it a noble Soul that the other covered;
" for when he attended the King, for the
" laft Time, he fhewed, he had a true
" Senfe of the Weight of his Charge. For
" as his Majefty was riding, he complain'd
" of

To the READER.

" of the Horse, *That it was the heaviest dull*
" *Jade he ever rode on.* To this *Penderell*,
" very senfibly, reply'd. — *My Liege! can*
" *you blame the Horse for going so heavily,*
" *when he has the Weight of the three King-*
" *doms on his Back.*

" WHEN I am in the Meditation of the
" many Paffages, that this little Hiftory re-
" counts, between the King and *Penderell*,
" my Attention is fo fixed to the melan-
" cholly Parts, which exercifed this Man's
" Fidelity, that the knowing of the Story
" to the End, does not fuddenly interrupt
" my ferious Thoughts, with the then fu-
" ture Glories of a Reftoration, that he was
" referved for, nor with the Wonders, that
" *Monk* was to perform.—I love to dwell a
" little upon the Fidelity of this good Man :
" It is a familiar Example, but it is the
" more ufeful; the leaft Man may be faith-
" ful, and Fidelity will make him great;
" but the greateft Man without Integrity,
" dwindles into a little one. — It is true,
" alfo, Integrity make a great Man greater;
" fo it is with General *Monk*, a Name far
" beyond his Title as Duke of *Albemarle.*
" Every one admires the *General* and the
" *Reftorer*; for my Share, it is a fingular
" Pleafure to me to dwell in Thought upon
" this

To the READER.

" this Subject only, 'till I conclude it, and
" to own publickly, how fondly I esteem
" and venerate this honest Countryman of
" ours, this Preserver of our King.

" A little Gentlemanly Estate was after-
" wards settled upon his Descendants for
" this Action; and had he been even ad-
" vanced by the Pleasure of the King, from
" that lowly Degree, to the Nobility, no
" Lord could have thonght himself polluted,
" by having for his Peer and Companion,
" the Heir of that worthy Man, who had
" the Honour to preserve, in so remakable
" a Manner, the Fountain of Honour it self.
" But, as it was, I know no greater En-
" couragement can be given to People of all
" Conditions to be faithful, than this Ex-
" ample, which a King of *England* has
" given of the Truth of what has been said
" by the wisest of Kings and Men : *He that*
" *loveth Pureness of Heart, for the Grace of*
" *his Lips, the King shall be his Friend.*"

The

*The Inscription upon the Tomb-Stone
of* RICHARD PENDERELL, *situate in
the Church-yard of St.* Giles's *in the
Fields*, near the *South-Eaſt* Corner
of the Church.

HERE lieth the Body of RICHARD
PENDERELL, Preſerver and
Conductor to His Sacred Majeſty King
CHARLES II. of *Great Britain*, after his
Eſcape from *Worceſter* Fight in the Year
1651, who died *Feb.* 8, 1671.

> *Hold, Paſſenger, here's ſhrouded in this
>   Herſe,*
>
> *Unparallell'd* PEND'RELL, *thro' the
>   Univerſe.*
>
> *Like when the Eaſtern Star from Heav'n
>   gave Light*
>
> *To three loſt Kings, ſo he, in ſuch dark
>   Night,*
>
> *To* Britain's *Monarch, loſt by adverſe
>   War,*
>
> *On Earth appear'd a ſecond Eaſtern
>   Star ;*
>
> *A Pole*

An Inscription, &c.

A Pole astern, in her rebellious Main,
A Pilot to her Royal Sovereign.
Now to triumph in Heav'n's eternal
Sphere,
He's hence advanc'd for his just Stee-
rage here;
Whilst Albion's Chronicle, with match-
less Fame,
Embalms the Story of Great PEN-
D'RELL's Name.

On a Piece of the ROYAL-OAK, sent to a Gentleman as a Tobacco-Stopper.

I Send you, Sir, this poor Remain of Wood,
Vile as it seems, 'tis venerably good:
It is a Fragment of that ancient Tree,
The ROYAL-OAK, Safeguard of Majesty;
Which has the Force of Wind and Weather stood,
Till Time decay'd this very Heart of Wood;
And tho' some abdicated Years have past,
Since that brave Stock shot out and sprouted last,
It still remains such in its Sacred Parts,
As those who truly suffer Loyal Hearts.

A SUM-

A
SUMMARY
OF THE
Royal PROGRESS,

From His Majesty's first Landing in *Scotland*, to His safe Arrival in *Paris*, Oct. 13, 1651.

CONTENTS.

                 —*Quarters*

CONTENTS.

CONTENTS.

B O S C O-

BOSCOBEL:

OR, THE

HISTORY

OF

King Charles II's

Most miraculous PRESERVATION
after the BATTEL *of*

WORCESTER, &c.

PART I.

I T was in *June*, in the Year 1650,
that CHARLES the II. undoubted
Heir to CHARLES the I. of Glorious Memory, *King of* GREAT-
BRITAIN, FRANCE, and IRELAND, (after
his *Royal Father* had been barbarously Murder'd, and himself Banish'd his own Dominions, by his own rebellious Subjects) took Ship-

B   ping

ping at *Scheevling* in *Holland*, and having escaped great Dangers at Sea, arrived soon after at *Spey* in the North of *Scotland*.

ON the 1st of *January* following, his Majesty was Crown'd at *Scoon*, and an Army raised in that Kingdom, to invade this; in hope to recover his Regalities here, then most unjustly detained from him, by some Members of the *Long-Parliament*, and *Oliver Cromwel* their General, who soon after most Traiterously assum'd the Title of *Protector* of the new-minted Common-wealth of *England, Scotland*, and *Ireland*.

OF this Royal *Scotch* Army the General Officers were these, Lieutenant General *David Lesley*, Lieutenant General *Middleton*, (who is since created Earl of *Middleton*, Lord *Clarmont*, and *Fettercairn*) Major General *Massey*, Major General *Montgomery*, Major General *Datiel*, and Major General *Vandrose*, a *Dutchman*.

THE 1st of *August*, 1651, his Majesty with his Army began his March into *England*, and on the 5th of the same Month at his Royal Camp at *Woodhouse* near the *Border*, published his Gracious Declaration of General Pardon and Oblivion to all his loving Subjects of the Kingdom of *England* and Dominion of *Wales*, that would desist from assisting the Usurped

Ufurped Authority of the pretended Common-wealth of *England*, and return to the obedience *they owed to their lawful King, and to the antient happy Government of the Kingdom*; except only *Oliver Cromwel, Henry Ireton, John Bradfhaw, John Cook*, (pretended Solicitor,) and all others who did actually fit and vote in the Murder of His *Royal Father*.

And laftly did declare, *That the Service being done the* Scotch *Army fhould quietly retire, that fo all Armies might be difbanded, and the lafting Peace fettled with Religion and Righteoufnefs*.

His Majefty after the Publication of this gracious Offer, march'd his Army into *Lancafhire*, where he received fome confiderable Supplies from the *Earl of Derby* (that loyal Subject,) and at *Warrington Bridge* met with the firft Oppofition made by the Rebels in *England*, but His Prefence foon put them to Flight.

In the Interim His Majefty had fent a Copy of his Declaration, inclofed in a Gracious Letter to *Thomas Andrews*, then Lord Mayor, (who had been one of His late Majefty's Judges) and the Aldermen of the City of *London*, which, by Order of the Rump-Rebels then fitting at *Weftminfter*, was (on the 26th of *Auguft*) publicly burnt at the Old

B 2 *Exchange*

Exchange by the Hangman; and their own Declaration Proclaimed there and at *Westminster*, with beat of Drum, and sound of Trumpet; by which His Sacred Majesty, (to whom they could afford no better Title then *Charles Stuart*) *His Abettors, Agents and Complices, were declared Traytors, Rebels and public Enemies.* Impudence and Treason beyond Example!

AFTER a tedious March of near three hundred Miles, His Majesty, with his Army, on the 22d of *August*, possessed himself of *Worcester*, after some small opposition made by the Rebels there, commanded by Colonel *John James*; and at His Entrance the Mayor of that City carried the Sword before his Majesty, who had left the Earl of *Derby* in *Lancashire*, as well to settle that and the adjacent Countries in a posture of Defence, against *Cromwel* and his Confederates; as to raise some Auxiliary Forces to recruit his Majesty's Army, in case the success of a Battel should not prove so happy as all good Men desired.

BUT (such was Heaven's Degree) on the 25th, of *August*, the Earl's new rais'd Forces, being over-power'd, were totally defeated near *Wiggan* in that County by Colonel *Lilburn*, with a Regiment of Rebellious Sectaries. In which conflict the Lord *Widdrington*, Sir

Thomas

Thomas Tildesly, Colonel *Trollop*, Colonel *Boin-ton*, Lieutenant Colonel *Galliard*, (faithful Sub-jects and Valiant Soldiers) with some others of good Note, were slain; Colonel *Edward Roscarrock* wounded, Sir *William Trockmorton*, (now Knight Marshal to His Majesty) Sir *Timothy Fetherstonhaugh*, (who was beheaded by the Rebels at *Chester*, on the 22d of *October* following) Colonel *Baines*, and others taken Prisoners, and their General the Earl of *Derby*, (who charged the Rebels Valiantly, and re-ceived several Wounds) put to flight with a small number of his Men: In which Condition he made choice of the way towards *Worcester*, whither he knew his Majesty's Army was de-sign'd to March.

AFTER some Days, my Lord, with Colo-nel *Roscarrock* and two Servants got into the confines of *Staffordshire* and *Shropshire* near *Newport*, where at one Mr. *Watson's* House he met with Mr. *Richard Snead*, (an honest Gentleman of that Country, and of his Lord-ship's Acquaintance) to whom he re-counted the Misfortune of his Defeat at *Wiggan*, and the Necessity of his taking some rest, if Mr. *Snead* could recommend his Lordship to any private House near hand, where he might safely continue, till he could find an Oppor-tunity to go to His Majesty.

MR.

Mr. *Snead* brought my Lord and his Company to *Boscobel-House*, a very obscure Habitation, scituate in *Shropshire*, but adjoining upon *Staffordshire*, and lies between *Tong-Castle* and *Brewood*, in a kind of Wilderness. *John Giffard*, Esq; having built this House about thirty Years since, invited Sir *Basil Brook* with other Friends and Neighbours to a House-warming Feast; at which time Sir *Basil* was desired by Mr. *Giffard* to give the House a Name, he aptly calls it BOSCOBEL (from the *Italian Bosco-bello*, which in that Language signifies *Fair-wood*) because seated in the midst of many fair Woods.

At this Place the Earl arriv'd on the 29*th*, of *August*, (being *Friday*) at Night, but the House at that time afforded no Inhabitant except *William Penderel*, the House-keeper and his Wife, who, to preserve so eminent a Person, freely adventur'd to receive my Lord, and kept him in safety till *Sunday* Night following, when (according to my Lord's desire of going to *Worcester*) he convey'd him to Mr. *Humphry Elliot*'s House at *Gataker-Park*, (a true hearted Royalist) which was about nine Miles on the way to *Boscobel* thither. Mr. *Elliot* did not only chearfully entertain the Earl, but lent him ten Pounds, and con-

ducted

ducted him and his Company safe to *Worcester.*

THE next Day after his Majesty's arrival at *Worcester,* being *Saturday* the 23d of *August,* he was Proclaimed King of GREAT-BRITAIN, FRANCE, and IRELAND, by Mr. *Thomas Lisens,* Mayor, and Mr. *James Bridges,* Sheriff of that loyal City, with great Acclamations.

ON the same Day his Majesty publish'd this following *Manifesto* or *Declaration.*

CHARLES *by the Grace of God, King of* ENGLAND, SCOTLAND, FRANCE, *and* IRELAND; *Defender of the Faith,* &c. *To all whom it may concern Greeting. We desire not the effusion of Blood, we covet not the spoil or forfeiture of our People, our Declaration at our entry into this Kingdom, the quiet Behaviour and Abstinence of our Army throughout this long March, and our general Pardon declared to all the Inhabitants of this City, without taking advantage of the opposition here made us, by a force of the Enemy over-mastering them, until we chased them away, have sufficiently certified both what we seek is only that the Laws of* ENGLAND *(which secure the right both of King and Subject) may henceforth recover their due power and force, and all past bitterness of*

these

*these unnatural Wars be buried and forgotten.
As a means whereunto, we have by our Warrants of the date hereof, and do hereby Summon,
upon their Allegiance, all the Nobility, Gentry,
and others of what degree and condition soever
of our County of* Worcester, *from sixteen to
sixty-to appear in their Persons, and with any
Horses, Arms and Ammunition they have or
can procure, at* Pitch-Croft, *near the City, on*
Tuesday *next being the 26th of this Instant
Month, where our self will be present that Day
(and also the next, in case those of the further
parts of the County should not be able to come
up sooner) to dispose of them as we shall think
fit, for our Service in the War, in defence of this
City and County, and to add unto our marching
Army, and to apply others (therein versed) to
matters of civil Advice and Government. Upon
which appearance we shall immediately Declare
to all present and conforming themselves to our
Royal Authority, our* Free Pardon, *not excluding from this Summons or the Pardon held
forth, or from trust and imployment in our service, as we shall find them cordial and useful
therein, any Person or Persons heretofore, or
at this time actually employ'd in opposition to us,
whether in the Military way, as Governors,
Colonels, Captains, Common Soldiers, or what-
soever else; or in the Civil as Sheriffs, under-*
Sheriffs,

Sheriffs, Juftices of the Peace, Collectors, High-Conftables, or any other higher or lower Quality; for fecuring of all whom before mentioned, in their loyal Addreffes, and performances, (befides our Army more then once fuccefsful fince our entrance) which will be between Them and the Enemy, and the engagement of our own Perfon in their defence,) we have directed this City to be forthwith fortified, and fhall ufe fuch other helps and means as fhall occur to us in order to that end: But on the other fide, if any Perfon of what Degree or Quality foever, either thro' Difloyalty, and Difaffection, or out of fear of the cruel Ufurpers, and Oppreffors, accompanied with a prefumption upon our Mercy and Goodnefs; or laftly, prefuming upon former Service, fhall oppofe, or neglect us at this Time, they fhall find, that as We have Authority to punifh in Life, Liberty and Eftate, fo we want not now Power to do it, and (if over much provoked) fhall not want the will neither, and in particular unto thofe who have heretofore done and fuffered for their Loyalty: We fay it is now in the Hands either to double that Score, or to ftrike it off; concluding with this, That altho' our difpofition abound with tendernefs to our People, yet we cannot think it fuch to let them lye under a confeft Slavery, and falfe Peace, when as we well know, and all the World may fee, we have force

enough

enough, with the conjunction of those that Groan under the present Yoak, (we will not say to dispute, for that we shall do well enough with those we have brought with us) but clearly (without any considerable opposition) to restore together with our self the Quiet, the Liberty, and the Laws of the English *Nation.*

GIVEN at our City of *WORCESTER* the 23d, of *August* 1651. and in the III. Year of our Reign.

UPON *Sunday* the 24th of *August,* Mr. *Crosby* (an eminent Divine of that City) Preached before his Majesty in the Cathederal Church; and in his Prayer, stiled his Majesty, *in all Causes, and over all Persons, next under God, Supreme Head and Governor :* At which the Presbyterian *Scots* took exception, and Mr. *Crosby* was afterwards admonished by some of them to forbear such expressions.

TUESDAY the 26th. of *August,* was the Rendevouz in *Pitchcroft* of such loyal Subjects as came to his Majesty's aid, in pursuance of his before-mentioned Declaration and Summons: Here appeared

Francis Lord *Talbot,* now Earl of *Shrewsbury* with about 60 Horse.

Mr.

Mr. *Mervin Touchet*, his Lieutenant Colonel.

Sir *John Packington.*

Sir *Walter Blount.*

Sir *Ralph Clare.*

Sir *Rowland Berkley.*

Sir *John Winford.*

Mr. *Ralph Sheldon* of *Beoly.*

Mr. *John Washburn* of *Witchinford*, with 40 Horse.

Mr. *Thomas Hornyold* of *Blackmore Park*, with 40 Horse.

Mr. *William Seldon* of *Finstall.*

Mr. *Thomas Acton.*

Captain *Benbow.*

Mr. *Robert Blount* of *Kenswick,*

Mr. *Robert Wigmore* of *Lucton.*

Mr. *Edward Pennel* the Elder.

Captain *Kingston.*

Mr. *Peter Blount.*

Mr. *Edward Blount.*

Mr. *Walter Walsh.*

Mr. *Charles Wash.*

Mr. *William Dansey.*

Mr. *Francis Knotsford.*

Mr. *George Chambers*, &c.

WITH divers others, who were honoured and encouraged by his Majesty's Presence: Notwithstanding which Access, the Number of of his Army both *English* and *Scots,* was conceived not to exceed 12,000 Men, *viz.* 10,000 *Scots,* and about 2000 *English* ; and those too not excellently armed, nor plentifully stored with Ammunition.

MEAN time *Cromwel* (that grand Patron of Sectaries) had amass'd together a numerous Body of Rebels, commanded by himself in Chief, and the Lord *Grey* of *Groby, Fleetwood* and *Lambert* under him, consisting of above 30,000 Men, (being generally the Scum and Froth of the whole Kingdom) one part of which were Sectaries, who, through a Fanatick Zeal were become *Devotes* to this great *Idol*; the other part seduc'd Persons, who either by force or fear were unfortunately made Actors or Participants in this so horrible and fatal a Tragedy.

THUS then began the Pickeerings to the grand Engagement, Major General *Massey* with a commanded Party, being sent by his Majesty to secure the Bridge and Pass at *Upton* upon *Severn,* seven Miles below *Worcester,* on *Thursday* the 28th of *August, Lambert* with a far greater number of Rebels attack'd him, and after some dispute gained the Pass, the River being then fordable. Yet the Major General behav'd himself very Gallantly, received a Shot in the Hand from some Musketiers

tiers the Enemy had conveyed into the Church, and retreated in good Order to *Worcester.*

DURING this Encounter, *Cromwell* himself, (whose Head-Quarter was the Night before at *Pershore*) advanc'd to *Stoughton,* within four Miles of the City on the South Side, himself quartered that Night at Mr. *Simons* House at *White Lady-Aston,* and a Party of his Horse faced the City that Evening.

THE next Day (*August* the 29th) *Sultan Oliver* appear'd with a great Body of Horse and Foot on *Red-Hill* within a Mile of *Worcester,* where he made a *Bonnemine,* but attempted nothing ; and that Night Part of his Army quartered at Judge *Barkley's* House at *Speachley.* The fame Day it was resolv'd by his Majesty at a Council of War, to give the Grand Rebel a *Camisado,* by beating up his Quarters that Night with 1500 select Horse and Foot, commanded by Lieutenant-General *Middleton,* and Sir *William Keyth* ; all of them wearing their Shirts over their Armour for distinction ; which accordingly was attempted, and might in all probability have been successful, had not the Design been most traiterously discover'd to the Rebels by one *Guyse* a Taylor in the

C Town,

Town, and a notorious Sectary, who was hang'd the Day following, as the just Reward of his Treachery: In this Action Major *Knox* was slain, and some few taken Prisoners by the Enemy. A considerable Party of the Rebels commanded by Colonel *Fleetwood*, Colonel *Richard Ingoldsby*, (who since became a real Convert, and was created Knight of the *Bath* at his Majesty's Coronation) Colonel *Goff*, and Colonel *Gibbons* being got over the *Severn* at *Upton*, march'd next Day to *Powick* Town, where they made an Halt, for *Powick-Bridge* (lying upon the River *Team*, between *Powick* Town and *Worcester*) was guarded by a Brigade of his Majesty's Horse and Foot, commanded by Major-General *Robert Montgomery*, and Colonel *George Keyth*.

The fatal 3d of *September* being come, his Majesty this Day (holding a Council of War upon the Top of the *College* Church Steeple, the better to discover the Enemies Posture) observed some Firing at *Powick*, and *Cromwell* making a Bridge of Boats over *Severn*, under *Buns-bill*, about a Mile below the City towards *Team* Mouth; his Majesty presently goes down, commands all to their Arms, and marches in Person to *Powick-Bridge*, to give Orders, as well for

main-

maintaining that Bridge, as for opposing the making the other of Boats, and hasted back to his Army in the City.

Soon after his Majesty was gone from *Powick-Bridge*, the Enemy assaulted it furiously, which was well defended by *Montgomery*, till himself was dangerously wounded, and his Ammunition spent; so that he was forced to make a disorderly Retreat into *Worcester*, leaving Colonel *Keyth* a Prisoner at the Bridge. At the same Time *Cromwell* had with much Celerity finish'd his Bridge of Boats and Planks over the main River, without any considerable Opposition; saving that Colonel *Piscotty*, with about three hundred Highlanders, performed as much therein as could be expected from a handful of Men fighting against great Numbers : By this means *Oliver* held Communication with those of his Party at *Powick-Bridge*, and when he had march'd over a considerable Number of his Men, said, (in his hypocritical Way) *The Lord of Hosts be with you*, and return'd himself to raise a Battery of great Guns against the *Fort-Royal* on the South-side of the River.

His Majesty being return'd from *Powick-Bridge*, march'd with the Duke of *Buckingham*, Lord *Grandison*, and some other of

his.

his Cavalry through the City, and out at *Sudbury-Gate* by the *Fort-Royal*, where the Rebels great Shot came frequently near his sacred Person.

At this Time *Cromwell* was settled in an advantageous Post at *Perry-wood*, within a Mile of the City, swelling with Pride, and confident in the Numbers of his Men, having besides rais'd a Breast-work at the Cockshoot of that Wood, for his greater Security; but Duke *Hamilton* (formerly Lord *Lanerick*) with his own Troop and some Highlanders, Sir *Alexander Forbes* with his Regiment of Foot, and divers *English* Lords and Gentlemen Voluntiers, by his Majesty's Command and Encouragement, engaged him, and did great Execution upon his best Men, forced the great *Sultan* (as the *Rhodians* in like Case did the *Turks*) to retreat with his *Janazaries*, and his Majesty was once as absolute Master of his great Guns, as he ought then to have been of the whole Land.

Here his Majesty gave an incomparable Example of Valour to the rest, by charging in Person, which the *Highlanders*, especially, imitated in a great Measure, fighting with the But-end of their Muskets, when their Ammunition was spent; but new Supplies

plies of Rebels being continually poured upon them, and the main Body of *Scotch*
Horse not coming up in due Time from the
Town to his Majesty's Relief, his Army
was forced to retreat in at *Sudbury* Gate in
much Disorder.

IN this Action Duke *Hamilton* (who
fought valiantly) had his Horse killed under him, and was himself mortally wounded, of which he died within few Days ;
and many of his Troop (consisting much of
Gentlemen, and diverse of his own Name)
were slain : Sir *John Douglass* received his
Death's Wound ; and Sir *Alexander Forbes,*
(who was the first Knight the King made in
Scotland, and commanded the *Fort Royal*
here) was shot through both the Calves of
his Legs, lay in the Wood all Night, and
was brought Prisoner to *Worcester* next
Day.

THE Rebels in this Encounter had great
Advantage, as well in their Numbers, as
by fighting both with Horse and Foot, a-
gainst his Majesty's Foot only, the greatest
Part of his Horse being wedged up in the
Town. And when the Foot were defeated, a Part of his Majesty's Horse fought
afterwards against both the Enemies Horse
and Foot upon great Disadvantage. And

as

as they had few Perſons of Condition among
them to loſe, ſo no Rebels, but Quarter-
maſter General *Moſely*, and one Captain
Jones, were worth taking Notice of to be
ſlain in the Battle.

At *Sudbury* Gate (I know not whether
by Accident, or on Purpoſe) a Cart laden
with Ammunition was overthrown and lay
a-croſs the Paſſage, one of the Oxen that
drew it being there killed, ſo that his Majeſty could not ride into the Town; but was
forced to diſmount and come in on Foot.

The Rebels ſoon after Stormed the *Fort
Royal* (the Fortifications whereof were not
perfected) and put all the *Scots* they found
therein to the Sword.

In the *Friars-Street* his Majeſty put off
his Armour, (which was heavy and trouble-
ſome to him) and took a freſh Horſe ; and
then perceiving many of his Foot Soldiers
began to throw down their Arms and de-
cline fighting, he rode up and down among
them, ſometimes with his Hat in his Hand,
entreating them to ſtand to their Arms, and
fight like Men ; other Whiles encouraging
them, alledging the Goodneſs and Juſtice
of the Cauſe they fought for ; but ſeeing
himſelf not able to prevail, ſaid, *I had rather you would ſhoot me, than keep me alive*

to see the sad Consequences of this fatal Day.
So deep a Sense had his prophetic Soul of
the Miseries of his beloved Country, even
in the midst of his own Danger.

During this hot Engagement at *Perry-
wood* and *Red-hill*, the Rebels on the other
Side the Water possessed themselves of S.
John's, and a Brigade of his Majesty's Foot
which were there, under the Command of
M. Gen. *Daliel*, without any great Resis-
tance, laid down their Arms and craved
Quarter.

When some of the Enemy were entred,
and entering the Town both at the *Key*,
Castle-hill and *Sudbury* Gate, without any
Conditions : The Earl of *Cleveland*, Sir
James Hamilton, Col. *Tho. Worgan*, Col.
William Carlis, (then Major to the Lord
Talbot) L. Col. *John Slaughter*, Capt. *Tho.
Hornyold*, Capt. *Tho. Giffard*, Capt. *John
Astley*, Mr. *Peter Blount*, and Capt. *Richard
Kemble* (Capt. Lieutenant to the Lord *Tal-
bot*) and some others rallied what Force they
could, (though inconsiderable to the Rebels
Numbers) and charged the Enemy very gal-
lantly both in *Sudbury-street* and *High-street*,
where Sir *James* and Capt. *Kemble* were de-
sperately wounded, and others slain ; yet
this Action did much secure his Majesty's

March

March out at St. *Marten*'s Gate, who had otherwise been in Danger of being taken in the 'Town.

About the same Time the Earl of *Rothes*, Sir *William Hamilton*, and Col. *Drummond*, with a Party of *Scots*, maintained the *Castle-Hill* with much Resolution, till such Time as Conditions were agreed on for Quarter.

Lastly, some of his Majesty's *English* Army valiantly opposed the Rebels at the Town Hall, where Mr. *Coningsby Colles*, and some others were slain, Mr. *John Rumney*, Mr. *Charles Wells*, and others, taken Prisoners; so that the Rebels having in the End subdued all their Opponents, fell to plundering the City unmercifully, few or none of the Citizens escaping, but such as were of the Phanatic Party.

When his Majesty saw no hope of rallying his thus discomfited Foot, he marched out of *Worcester* at St. *Martin*'s Gate, (the fore Gate being mured up) about six of the Clock in the Evening, with his main Body of Horse, as then commanded by General *David Lesley*, but were now in some Confusion.

The Lord-St. *Clare*, with divers of the *Scottish* Nobility and Gentry, were taken

Prisoners

Prifoners in the Town. And the Foot Soldiers (confifting moft of *Scots*) were almoft
either flain or taken, and fuch of them (who
in the Battle efcaped Death) lived but longer to die, for the moft Part, more mife-
rably ; many of them being afterwards
knock'd o'the Head by Country People ;
fome bought and fold like Slaves for a fmall
Price, others went begging up and down,
till Charity failing them, their Neceffities
brought upon them Difeafes, and Difeafes,
Death.

BEFORE his Majefty was come to *Bar-
bon's* Bridge, about half a Mile out of
Worcefter, he made feveral Stands, faced
about, and defired the Duke of *Bucking-
bam,* Lord *Wilmot,* and other of his Commanders, that they might rally and try the
Fortune of War once more : But at the Bridge
a ferious Confultation was held, and then
perceiving many of the Troopers to throw
off their Arms, and fhift for themfelves, they
were all of Opinion, the Day was irrecove-
rably loft, and that their only remaining
Work was to fave the King from thofe ravenous Wolves and Regicides : Whereupon
his Majefty by Advice of his Council, refolv'd to march with all Speed for *Scotland,*
following therein the Steps of King *David*
his

his great Predeceffor in Royal Patience, who finding himfelf in Circumftances not unlike to thefe, *faid to all his Servants that were with him at* Jerufalem, *Arife, and*

2 Sam. *let us fly, for we fhall not elfe ef-*

XV. 14. *cape from* Abfolom, *make fpeed to depart, left he overtake us fuddenly, and bring Evil upon us, and fmite the City with the Edge of the Sword.*

IMMEDIATELY after this Refu't, the Duke asked the Lord *Talbot,* (being of that Country) if he could direct the Way Northwards? His Lordfhip anfwered, that he had one *Richard Walker* in his Troop (formerly a Scout-mafter in thofe Parts, and who fince died in *Jamaica*) that knew the Way well; who was accordingly called to be the Guide, and performed that Duty for fome Miles; but being come to *Kinver-Heath,* not far from *Kederminfter,* and Day-light being gone, *Walker* was at a puzzle in the Way.

HERE his Majefty made a Stand, and confulted with the Duke, Earl of *Derby,* Lord *Wilmot,* &c. To what Place he might march, at leaft to take fome Hours Reft; the Earl of *Derby* told his Majefty, that in his Flight from *Wiggan* to *Worcefter,* he had met with a perfect honeft Man, and a great

Con-

Convenience of Concealment at *Boscobel-House*, (before-mentioned) but withal acquainted the King, it was a Recusants House; and it was suggested, that those People (being accustomed to Persecution and Searches) were most like to have the readiest Means, and safest Contrivances to preserve him; his Majesty therefore inclined to go thither.

THE Lord *Talbot* being made acquainted therewith, and finding *Walker* dubious of the Way, called for Mr. *Charles Giffard*, (a faithful Subject, and of the antient Family of *Chillington*) to be his Majesty's Conducter, which Office Mr. *Giffard* willingly undertook, having one *Yates* a Servant with him, very expert in the Ways of that Country; and being come near *Sturbridge*, it was under Consideration, whether his Majesty should march through that Town or no, and resolved in the affirmative, and that all about his Person should speak *French* to prevent any Discovery of his Majesty's Presence.

MEAN Time General *Lesley* with the *Scottish* Horse, had in the close of the Evening, taken the more direct Way Northward by *Newport*, his Majesty being left only attended by the Duke of *Buckingham*, Earl of *Derby*, Earl of *Lauderdale*, Lord *Talbot*,

Talbot, Lord *Wilmot*, Col. *Thomas Blague*, Col. *Edward Roscarrock*, Mr. *Marmaduke Darey*, Mr. *Richard Lane*, Mr. *William Armorer*, (since Knighted) Mr. *Hugh May*, Mr. *Charles Giffard*, Mr. *Peter Street*, and some others, in all about 60 Horse.

At a House about a Mile beyond *Sturbridge*, his Majesty drank, and eat a Crust of Bread, the House affording no better Provision; and as his Majesty rode on, he discoursed with Col. *Roscarrock* touching *Boscobel-House*, and the Means of Security, which the Earl of *Derby* and he found at that Place.

However Mr. *Giffard* humbly proposed to carry his Majesty first to *White-Ladies*, (another Seat of the *Giffard's*) lying but half a Mile beyond *Boscobel*, where he might repose himself for a while, and then take such further Resolution, as his Majesty and Council should think fit.

This House is distant about 26 Miles from *Worcester*, and still retains the antient Name of *White-Ladies*, from its having formerly been a Monastery of *Cistertian* Nuns, whose Habit was of that Colour.

His Majesty and his Retinue (being safely conducted thither by Mr. *Giffard*) alighted, now, as they hoped, out of Danger
ger

ger of any prefent Surprife by Purfuits, *George Penderel* (who was a Servant in the Houfe) opened the Doors; and after his Majefty and the Lords were entered the Houfe, his Majefty's Horfe was brought into the Hall, and by this Time it was about Break of Day on *Thurfday* Morning. Here every one was in a fad Confult how to efcape the Fury of blood-thirfty Enemies; but the greateft Solicitude was to fave the King, who was both hungry and tired with this long and hafty March.

Mr. *Giffard* prefently fent for *Richard Penderel,* who liv'd near Hand at *Hobbal Grange,* and Col. *Rofcarrock* caufed *Bartholomew Martin,* a Boy in the Houfe, to be fent to *Bofcobel* for *William Penderel,* mean Time Miftrefs *Giffard* brought his Majefty fome Sack and Bisket; for *the King and all the People that were with him, came weary and refrefhed themfelves there:* Richard came 2 Sam. xvi. 14. firft, and was immediately fent back to bring a Suit of his Cloaths for the King, and, by that Time he arrived with them, *William* came, and both were brought into the Parlour to the Earl of *Derby,* who immediately carried them into an inner Parlour (where the King was) and told

D

William

William Penderel, This is the King (pointing to his Majesty) *thou must have a Care of him, and preserve him as thou didst me:* And Mr. *Giffard* did also much conjure *Richard* to have a special Care of his Charge, to which Commands the two Brothers yielded ready Obedience.

WHILST *Richard* and *William* were thus sent for, his Majesty had been advised to rub his Hands on the Back of the Chimney, and with them his Face, for a Disguise, and some Person had disorderly cut off his Hair. His Majesty having put off his Garter, blue Ribband, George of Diamonds, Buff-Coat, and other princely Ornaments, committed his Watch to the Custody of the Lord *Wilmot*, and his George to Col. *Blague*, and distributed the Gold he had in his Pocket among his Servants, and then put on a noggen coarse Shirt which was borrowed of *Edward Martin*, who liv'd in the House, and *Richard Penderel*'s green Suit, and leather Doublet, but had not Time to be so disguised, as he was afterwards; for both *William* and *Richard Penderel* did advertise the Company to make Haste away, in Regard, there was a Troop of Rebels commanded by Col. *Ashenhurst*, quartered at *Cotsal*, but three Miles distant; some

some of which Troop came to the House within half an Hour after the Dissolution of the Royal Troop. *Thus* David *and his Men departed out of* Kei-   1 Sam. lah, *and went whithersoever they*   xxiii. 13. *could go.*

Richard Penderel conducted the King out at a Back-door, unknown to most of the Company (except some of the Lords and Colonel *Roscarrock*, who with sad Hearts, but hearty Prayers, took Leave of him) and carried him into an adjacent Wood belonging to *Boscobel* called *Spring-Coppice*, about half a Mile from *Whitela-dies* (where *he abode* as David did *in the Wilderness of* Ziph, *in a*   1 Sam. *Wood*) whilst *William, Humphrey*   xxiii. 15. and *George*, were scouting abroad to bring what News they could learn to his Majesty in the *Coppice*, as Occasion required.

His Majesty being thus, as they hoped, in a Way of Security, the Duke, Earl of *Derby*, Earl of *Lauderdale*, Lord *Talbot*, and the rest (having Mr. *Giffard* for their Guide, and being then not above forty Horse, of which Number his Majesty's Pad-nag was one, ridden by Mr. *Richard Lane*, one of the Grooms of the Bed-cham-

D 2   ber)

ber) marched from *Whiteladies* Northwards
by the Way of *Newport,* in hope to overtake or meet General *Lefley* with the main
Body of *Scotch* Horse.

As foon as they were got into the Road,
the Lord *Leviston* (who commanded his
Majefty's Life-guard) overtook them, purfued by a Party of Rebels under the Command of Col. *Blundel;* the Lords with their
Followers faced about, fought, and repell'd
them ; but when they came a little beyond
Newport, fome of Col. *Lilburn's* Men met
them in the Front, other Rebels, from *Worcester,* purfued in the Rear, themfelves and Horfes being fufficiently tired, the Earl of *Derby,*
Earl of *Lauderdale,* Mr. *Charles Giffard,*
and fome others were taken and carried
Prifoners, firft to *Whitchurch,* and from
thence to an Inn in *Bunbury* in *Chefhire,*
where Mr. *Giffard* found Means to make an
Efcape ; but the noble Earl of *Derby* was
thence conveyed to *Weftchefter,* and there
tried by a pretended Court Martial, held
the firft of *October* 1651, by Vertue of a
Commiffion from *Cromwell,* grounded on
an execrable *Rump-Act,* of the 12th of
Auguft, then laft paft, the very Title
whereof cannot be mentioned without Hor-
ror ; but it pretended moft traiteroufly to *pro-
hibit*

bibit Correspondence with Charles Stuart *(their lawful Sovereign) under Penalty of High-Treason, Loss of Life and Estate* —— *Prodigious Rebels!*

In this Black Tribunal *there sate, as Judges these Persons, and under these Titles.*

Col. *Humphrey Mackworth*, President.

Major-General *Mitton.*
Colonel *Robert Duckenfield.*
Colonel *Henry Bradshaw.*
Colonel *Thomas Croxton.*
Colonel *George Twisleton.*
Lieutenant-Colonel *Henry Birkenheal.*
Lieutenant-Colonel *Simon Finch.*
Lieutenant-Colonel *Alexander Newton.*
Captain *James Stepford.*
Captain *Samuel Smith.*
Captain *John Downs.*
Captain *Vincent Corbet.*
Captain *John Delves.*
Captain *John Griffith.*
Captain *Thomas Portington.*
Captain *Edward Alcock.*
Captain *Ralph Pownall.*

Captain

Captain *Richard Grantham.*
Captain *Edward Stelfax.*

Their Cruel Sentence.

Resolved by the Court upon the Question.

That JAMES *Earl of* Derby *is guilty of the Breach of the Act of the* 12th *of August* 1651, *last pass, entituled,* An Act prohibiting Correspondence with CHARLES STUART, *or his Party, and so of High-Treason against the Commonwealth of England, and is therefore worthy of Death.*

Resolved by the Court.

That the said JAMES *Earl of* Derby *is a Traitor to the Commonwealth of England, and an Abetter, Encourager and Assister of the declared Traitors and Enemies thereof, and shall be put to Death by severing his Head from his Body at the Market Place in the Town of* Boulton *in* Lancashire, *upon* Wednesday *the* 15th *Day of this Instant October, about the Hour of One of the Clock the same Day.*

THIS

THIS was the Authority, and some of these the Persons that so barbarously, and contrary to the Law of Nations, condemned this noble Earl to Death, notwithstanding his just Plea, *That he had Quarter for Life given him by one Captain Edge, who took him Prisoner.* But this could not obtain Justice, nor any Intercession, Mercy; so that on the 15th of the said *October,* he was accordingly beheaded at *Boulton,* in a most barbarous and inhumane Manner *.

THE Earl of *Lauderdale,* with several others, were carried Prisoners to the Tower, and afterwards to *Windsor Castle,* where they continued divers Years.

WHILST the Rebels were plundering those noble Persons, the Duke, with the Lord *Leviston,* Col. *Blague,* Mr. *Marmaduke Darcy,* and Mr. *Hugh May,* forsook the Road first, and soon after their Horses, and betook themselves to a By-way, and got into *Bloore* Park, near *Cheswardine,* about five Miles from *Newport,* where they

---

* *See the Proceedings against him at large; with his Prayers before his Death, and his Speech and courageous Deportment on the Scaffold.* In England's Black Tribunal, 5th Edit. p. 156, &c.

received

received fome Refrefhment at a little obfcure Houfe of Mr. *George Barlows*, and afterwards met with two honeft Labourers, in an adjoining Wood, to whom they communicated the Exigent and Diftrefs, which the Fortune of War had reduced them to, and finding them like to prove faithful, the Duke thought fit to imitate his Royal Mafter, delivered his *George* (which was given him by the Queen of *England*) to Mr. *May* (who preferved it through all Difficulties, and afterwards reftored it to his Grace in *Holland*) and changed Habit with one of the Workmen; and in this Difguife, by the Affiftance of Mr. *Barlow* and his Wife, was, after fome Days, conveyed by one *Nich. Matthews*, a Carpenter, to the Houfe of Mr. *Hawley*, an hearty Cavalier, at *Bilftrop* in *Nottinghamfhire*, from thence to the Lady *Villiers* Houfe at *Booksby* in *Leicefterfhire*; and after many Hardfhips and Encounters, his Grace got fecure to *London*, and from thence to his Majefty in *France*.

At the fame Time the Lord *Levifton*, Col. *Blague*, Mr. *Darcy*, and Mr. *May*, all quitted their Horfes, difguifed themfelves, and feverally fhifted for themfelves, and fome of them, through various Dangers

and

and Sufferings, contrived their Escapes; in particular, Mr. *May* was forced to lie twenty one Days in a Hay-mow belonging to one *John Bold*, an honest Husbandman, who liv'd at *Soudley*; *Bold* having all that Time Rebel Soldiers quartered in his House, yet failed not to give a constant Relief to his more welcome Guest; and when the Coast was clear of Soldiers, Mr. *May* came to *London* on Foot in his Disguise.

THE Lord *Talbot* (seeing no hope of rallying) hasted towards his Father's House at *Longford* near *Newport*, where being arrived, he conveyed his Horse into a neighbouring Barn, but was immediately pursued by the Rebels, who found the Horse sadled, and by that concluded my Lord not to be far off, so that they searched *Longford* House narrowly, and some of them continued in it four or five Days; during all which Time my Lord was in a close Place in one of the Out-houses, almost stifled for want of Air, and had perished for want of Food, had he not been once relieved in the Dead of the Night, and with much Difficulty, by a trusty Servant; yet his Lordship thought it a great Providence, even by these Hardships, to escape the Fury of such

Enemies,

Enemies, who fought the Destruction of the Nobility, as well as of their King.

IN this Interim the valiant Earl of *Cleveland*, who being above sixty Years of Age, had marched twenty-one Days together upon a trotting Horse) had also made his Escape from *Worcester*, when all the fighting Work was over, and was got to *Woolcot* in *Shropshire*, whither he was pursued, and taken at, or near Mistress *Broughton's* House, from whence he was carried Prisoner to *Stafford*, and from thence to the Tower of *London*.

COLONEL *Blague*, remaining at Mr. *Barlow's* House at *Bloor-pipe*, about eight Miles from *Stafford*, his first Action was, with Mrs. *Barlow's* Privity and Advice, to hide his Majesty's *George* under a Heap of Chips and Dust ; yet the Colonel could not conceal himself so well, but that he was here, soon after, taken and carried Prisoner to *Stafford*, and from thence conveyed to the Tower of *London*; mean Time the *George* was transmitted to Mr. *Robert Milward* of *Stafford* for better Security ; who afterwards faithfully conveyed it to Col. *Blague* in the Tower, by the trusty Hands of Mr *Isaac Walton* ; and the Colonel not long after happily escaping thence, restor'd

it

it to his Majefty's own Hands, which had been thus wonderfully preferved from being made a Prize to fordid Rebels.

The *Scotch Cavalry* (having no Place to retreat unto nearer than *Scotland*) were foon after difperfed, and moft of them taken by the Rebels and Country People in *Chefhire*, *Lancafhire*, and Parts adjacent.

Thus was this *Royal Army* totally fubdued; thus difperfed; and if in this fo important an Affair, any of the *Scottifh* Commanders were treacherous at *Worcefter*, (as fome fufpected) he has a great Account to make for the many Years Miferies that enfued thereby to both Nations, under the tyrannical, ufurped Government of *Cromwell.*

But to return to the Duty of my Attendance on his facred Majefty in *Spring-Coppice*; by that Time *Richard Penderel* had conveyed him into the obfcureft Part of it, it was about Sun-rifing on *Thurfday* Morning, and the Heavens wept bitterly at thefe Calamities; infomuch as the thickeft Tree in the Wood was not able to keep his Majefty dry, nor was there any Thing for him to fit on; wherefore *Richard* went to *Francis Tates* Houfe (a trufty Neighbour, who married his Wife's Sifter) where

he

he borrowed a Blanket, which he folded and laid on the Ground under a Tree for his Majesty to sit on.

At the same Time *Richard* spoke to the good-wife *Yates*, to provide some Victuals, and bring it into the Wood at a Place he appointed her: She presently made ready a Mess of Milk, and some Butter and Eggs, and brought them to his Majesty in the Wood; who being a little surprized to see the Woman (no good Concealer of a Secret) said chearfully to her; *Good Woman, can you be faithful to a distressed Cavalier?* She answered, *Yes, Sir, I will rather die than discover you*; with which Answer his Majesty was well satisfied; and received from her Hands, as David *did from* Abigails, *that which she brought him.*

1 Sam.
xxv. 35.

The Lord *Wilmot*, in the Interim took *John Penderel* for his Guide, but knew not determinately whither to go, purposing at first to have marched Northwards; but as they passed by *Brewood Forge*, the Forgemen made after them, till being told by one *Rich. Dutton*, that it was Col. *Crompton* whom they pursued, the *Vulcans* happily, upon that Mistake, quitted the Chase.

Soon

SOON after they narrowly escaped a Party of Rebels as they passed by *Covenbrook* ; so that seeing Danger on every Side, and *John* meeting with *William Walker* (a trusty Neighbour) committed my Lord to his Care and Counsel, who for the present conveyed them into a dry Marl-Pit, where they stay'd a While, and afterwards to one Mr. *Huntbache*'s House at *Brinsford*, and put their Horses into *John Evan*'s Barn, while *John Penderel* goes to *Wolverhampton*, to see what Convenience he could find for my Lord's coming thither ; but met with none, the Town being full of Soldiers.

YET *John* leaves no Means unessayed, hastens to *Northcot* (an adjacent Village) and there, whilst he was talking with goodwife *Underhill* (a Neighbour) in the Instant Mr. *John Huddleston* (a Sojourner at Mr. *Thomas Whitgreaves* of *Moseley*, and of *John*'s Acquaintance) was accidentally passing by, to whom *John* (well assured of his Integrity) presently addresses himself and his Business, relates to him the sad News of the Defeat of his Majesty's Army at *Worcester*, and discovers in what Strait and Confusion he had left his Majesty, and his Followers, at *Whiteladies*, and in particular, that he had brought thence a Per-

E

son of Quality (for *John* then knew not who my Lord was) to *Huntbaches* House, who, without present Relief, would be in great Danger of being taken.

MR. *Huddleston* goes home forthwith, takes *John* with him, and acquaints Mr. *Whitgreave* with the Business, who freely resolved to venture all, rather than such a Person should miscarry.

HEREUPON Mr. *Whitgreave* repairs to *Huntbaches* House, speaks with my Lord, and gives Direction how he should be privately conveyed into his House at *Moseley*, about ten of the Clock at Night; and though it so fell out, that the Directions were not punctually observed, yet my Lord and his Man were at last brought into the House where Mr. *Whitgreave* (after some Refreshment given them) conveys them into a secret Place, which my Lord admiring for its excellent Contrivance, and solicitous for his Majesty's Safety, said, *I would give a World my Friend* (meaning the King) *were here;* and then (being abundantly satisfied of Mr. *Whitgreave's* Fidelity) deposited in his Hands a little Bag of Jewels, which my Lord received again at his Departure.

As

As soon as it was Day, Mr. *Whitgreave* sent *William Walker* with my Lord's Horses to his Neighbour Col. *John Lane* of *Bentley*, near *Walsall*, South-east from *Moseley* about four Miles (whom Mr. *Whitgreave* knew to be a right honest Gentleman, and ready to contribute any Assistance to so charitable a Work) and wished *Walker* to acquaint the Colonel, that they belonged to some eminent Person about the King, whom he could better secure than the Horses: The Colonel willingly receives them and sends Word to Mr. *Whitgreave* to meet him that Night in a Close not far from *Moseley*, in order to the Tender of farther Service to the Owner of the Horses, whose Name neither the Colonel nor Mr. *Whitgreave* then knew.

On *Thursday* Night, when it grew dark, his Majesty resolved to go from those Parts into *Wales*, and to take *Richard Penderel* with him for his Guide; but, before they began their Journey, his Majesty went into *Richard's* House at *Hobbal Grange*, where the old good-wife *Penderel* had not only the Honour to see his Majesty, but to see him attended by her Son *Richard*. Here his Majesty had Time and Means better to complete his Disguise. His

Name

Name was agreed to be *Will. Jones*, and his Arms a Wood-Bill. In this Posture about nine a Clock at Night (after some Refreshment taken in the House) his Majesty, with his trusty Servant *Richard*, began their Journey on Foot, resolving to go that Night to *Madely* in *Shropshire*, about five Miles from *Whiteladies*, and within a Mile of the River *Severn*, over which their Way lay for *Wales*; in this Village lived one Mr. *Francis Woolf*, an honest Gentleman of *Richard*'s Acquaintance.

His Majesty had not been long gone, but the Lord *Wilmot* sent *John Penderel* from Mr. *Whitgreave*'s to *Whiteladies* and *Boscobel*, to know in what Security the King was, *John* returned and acquainted my Lord, that his Majesty was marched from thence. Hereupon my Lord began to consider which Way himself should remove with Safety.

Col. *Lane*, having secured my Lord's Horses, and being come to *Mosely* according to Appointment, on *Friday* Night, was brought up to my Lord by Mr. *Whitgreave*, and (after mutual Salutation) acquainted him, that his Sister Mrs. *Jane Lane*, had by Accident procured a Pass from some Commander of the Rebels, for

her

her felf and a Man to go a little beyond
Briftol, to fee Mrs. *Norton*, her fpecial
Friend, then near her Time of lying in;
and freely offer'd, if his Lordfhip thought
fit, he might make ufe of it, which my
Lord feemed inclinable to accept; and on
Saturday Night was conducted by Colonel
Lane's Man (himfelf not being well) to
the Colonel's Houfe at *Bentley*; his Lordfhip then, and not before, difcovering his
Name to Mr. *Whitgreave*, and giving him
many Thanks for fo great a Kindnefs in fo
imminent a Danger.

BEFORE his Majefty came to *Madely*,
he met with an ill-favoured Encounter at
Evelin Mill, being about two Miles from
thence. The Miller (it feems) was an honeft Man, but his Majefty and *Richard*
knew it not, and had then in his Houfe
fome confiderable Perfons of his Majefty s
Army, who took Shelter there in their
Flight from *Worcefter*, and had not been
long in the Mill; fo that the Miller was
upon his Watch, and *Richard* unhappily
permitting a Gate to clap, through which
they paffed, gave Occafion to the Miller to
come out of the Mill and boldly ask, *Who
is there?* *Richard* thinking the Miller had
purfued them, quitted the ufual Way in

E 3 fome

as

apprehended

in the

Place for

into a

lefs liable to the

his Majefty

continued in a Hay-

Mow

Mow there all the Day following, his Servant *Richard* attending him.

DURING his Majesty's Stay in the Barn, Mr. *Woolf* had often Conference with him about his intended Journey, and in order thereto took Care, by a trusty Servant (sent abroad for that Purpose) to inform himself more particularly of those Guards upon *Severn*, and had certain Word brought him, that not only the Bridges were secured, but all the Passage-Boats seized on; insomuch that he conceived it very hazardous for his Majesty to prosecute his Design for *Wales*, but rather go to *Boscobel-House*, being the most retired Place for Concealment in all the Country, and to stay there till an Opportunity of a farther safe Conveyance could be found out; which Advice his Majesty inclined to approve: And thereupon resolved for *Boscobel* the Night following; in the mean Time, his Hands not appearing sufficiently discoloured, suitable to his other Disguise, Mrs. *Woolf* provided Walnut-Tree Leaves, as the readiest expedient for that Purpose.

THE Day being over, his Majesty adventured to come again into the House, where having for some Time refreshed himself, and being furnished with Conveniences

niences for his Journey (which was conceived to be fafer on Foot than by Horfe) he, with his faithful Guide *Richard*, about eleven a-Clock at Night, fet forth toward *Bofcobel.*

ABOUT three of the Clock on *Saturday* Morning, being come near the Houfe, *Richard* left his Majefty in the Wood, whilft he went in to fee if any Soldiers were there, or other Danger; where he found Col. *William Carlis* (who had not feen, not the laft Man born, but the laft Man killed at *Worcefter*, and) who having with much Difficulty, made his Efcape from thence, was got into his own Neighbourhood, and for fome Time concealing himfelf in *Bofcobel-wood*, was come that Morning to the Houfe to get fome Relief of *William Penderel* his old Acquaintance.

Richard having acquainted the Colonel, that the King was in the Wood, the Colonel, with *William* and *Richard*, went prefently thither to give their Attendance, where they found his Majefty fitting on the Root of a Tree, who was glad to fee the Colonel, and came with them into the Houfe, where he eat Bread and Cheefe heartily, and (as an extraordinary) *William Penderel*'s Wife made his Majefty a

Poffet

Poſſet of thin Milk and ſmall Beer, and got ready ſome warm Water to waſh his Feet not only extreme dirty, but much galled with Travel.

The Colonel pulled off his Majeſty's Shoes, which were full of Gravel, and Stockings which were very wet, and there being no other Shoes in the Houſe that would fit him, the Good-Wife put ſome hot Embers in thoſe to dry them, whilſt his Majeſty's Feet were waſhing and his Stockings ſhifted.

Being thus a little refreſhed, the Colonel perſuaded his Majeſty to go back into the Wood) (ſuppoſing it ſafer than the Houſe) where the Colonel made choice of a thick leaved Oak, into which *William* and *Richard* helped them both up, and brought them ſuch Proviſion as they could get, with a Cuſhion for his Majeſty to ſit on; the Colonel humbly deſired his Majeſty (who had taken little or no Reſt the two preceding Nights) to ſeat himſelf as eaſily as he could in the Tree, and reſt his Head on the Colonel's Lap, who was watchful that his Majeſty might not fall. In this Oak they continued moſt Part of that Day; and in that Poſture his Majeſty ſlumbered away ſome

Part

Part of the Time, and bore all thefe Hardfhips and Afflictions with incomparable Patience,

In the Evening they returned to the
Houfe, where *William Penderel* acquainted
his Majefty with the fecret Place, wherein
the Earl of *Derby* had been fecured, which
his Majefty liked fo well, that he refolved,
whilft he ftay'd there, to truft only to that,
and go no more into the *Royal Oak*, as
from hence it muft be called, where he
could not fo much as fit at Eafe.

His Majefty now finding himfelf in a
hopeful Security, permitted *William Penderel* to fhave him, and cut the Hair off his
Head, as fhort at Top as the Sciffars would
do it, but leaving fome about the Ears, according to the Country Mode; Colonel
Carlis attending, told his Majefty, *William
was but a mean Barber*; To which his Majefty anfwered, *He had never been fhaved
by any Barber before.* The King bad *William* burn the Hair which he cut off, but
William was only difobedient in that, for
he kept a good Part of it, wherewith he
has fince pleafured fome Perfons of Honour, and is kept as a civil Relique.

Humphrey Penderel was this *Saturday* defigned to go to *Shefnal*, to pay fome Taxes

to one Captain *Broadway*; at whose House
he met with a Colonel of the Rebels, who
was newly come from *Worcester* in Purfuit
of the King, and who, being informed
that his Majefty had been at *Whiteladies*,
and that *Humphrey* was a near Neighbour
to the Place, examined. him ftrictly, and
laid before him, as well the Penalty for
concealiug the King, which was Death
without Mercy; as the Reward for difcovering him, which fhould be one thoufand
Pounds certain Pay. But neither fear of
Punifhment, nor hope of Reward, was a-
ble to tempt *Humphrey* into any Difloyalty;
he pleaded Ignorance, and was difmiffed;
and on *Saturday* Night related to his Majefty and the loyal Colonel at *Bofcobel*,
what had paffed betwixt him and the Rebel Colonel at *Shefnal.*

THIS Night the Good-Wife (whom his
Majefty was pleafed to call, *My Dame
Joan)* provided fome Chickens for his Majefty's Supper (a Dainty he had not lately
been acquainted with) and a little Pallet
was put into the fecret Place for his Majefty to reft in; fome of the Brothers being
continually upon Duty, watching the Ave-
nues of the Houfe, and the Road-way, to
prevent the Danger of a Surprife.

AFTER

AFTER Supper Colonel *Carlis* asked his Majesty, What Meat he would please to have provided for the Morrow, being *Sunday?* His Majesty desired some Mutton, if it might be had: But it was thought dangerous for *William* to go to any Market to buy it; since his Neighbours all knew he did not use to buy such for his own Diet, and so it might beget a Suspicion of his having Strangers at his House: But the Colonel found another Expedient to satisfy his Majesty's Desires; early on *Sunday* Morning he repairs to Mr. *William Staunton's* Sheep-Coat, who rented some of the Demeans of *Boscobel*; here he chose one of the best Sheep, sticks him with his Dagger, then sends *William* for the Mutton, who brings him home on his Back.

ON *Sunday* Morning (*September* the seventh) his Majesty got up early (his Dormitory being none of the best, nor his Bed the easiest) and, near the secret Place where he lay, had the Convenience of a Gallery to walk in, where he was observed to spend some Time in his Devotions, and where he had the Advantage of a Window, which surveyed the Road from *Tong* to *Brewood*. Soon after his Majesty coming down into the Parlour, his Nose fell a bleeding, which

put

put his poor faithful Servants into a great Fright; but his Majesty was pleased soon to remove it, by telling them, It often did so.

As soon as the Mutton was cold, *William* cut it up and brought a Leg of it into the Parlour; his Majesty called for a Knife and a Trencher, and cut some of it into Collops, and pricked them with the Knife Point; then called for a Frying-Pan and Butter, and fry'd the Collops himself, of which he eat heartily; Colonel *Carlis* the while being but Under-Cook (and that Honour enough too) made the Fire, and turned the Collops in the Pan.

When the Colonel afterwards attended his Majesty in *France*, his Majesty calling to Remembrance this Passage among others, was pleased merrily to propose it, as a problematical Question; Whether himself or the Colonel were the Master-Cook at *Boscobel*; and the Supremacy was of right adjudged to his Majesty.

All this while the other Brothers of the *Penderels* were in their several Stations, either scouting abroad to learn Intelligence, or upon some other Service; but it so pleased God, that, though the Soldiers had some Intelligence of his Majesty's having

F   been

been at *Whiteladies*, and none, that he was gone thence, yet this House (which proved a happy Sanctuary for his Majesty in this sad Exigent) had not at all been searched during his Majesty's Abode there, though that had several Times; this, perhaps, the rather escaping, because the Neighbours could rather inform, none but poor Servants lived here.

His Majesty spent some Part of this Lord's-Day in Reading in a pretty Arbour in *Boscobel* Garden, which grew upon a Mount, and wherein there was a Stone Table, and Seats about it; and commended the Place for its Retiredness.

And having understood by *John Penderel*, that the Lord *Wilmot* was at Mr. *Whitgreave*'s House (for *John* knew not of his Remove to *Bentley)* his Majesty was desirous to let my Lord hear of him, and that he intended to come to *Mosely* that Night.

To this End *John* was sent on *Sunday* Morning to *Moseley*; but, finding my Lord removed thence, was much troubled, and then acquainting Mr. *Whitgreave* and Mr. *Huddleston*, that his Majesty was returned to *Boscobel*, and the Disaccommodation he had there; whereupon they both resolve to go with *John* to *Bentley*, where having
gained

gained him an Acceſs to my Lord, his Lordſhip deſigned to attend the King that Night at *Moſeley*, and deſired Mr. *Whitgreave* to meet his Lordſhip at a Place appointed about twelve of the Clock, and Mr. *Huddleſton* to nominate a Place where he would attend his Majeſty about one of the Clock the ſame Night.

Upon this Intelligence my Lord made Stay of Mrs. *Jane Lane*'s Journey to *Briſtol*, till his Majeſty's Pleaſure was known.

John Penderel return'd to *Boſcobel* in the Afternoon with Intimation of this deſign'd meeting with my Lord at *Moſeley* that Night; and the Place which was appointed by Mr. *Huddleſton*, where his Majeſty ſhould be expected. But his Majeſty, having not recovered his late Foot-Journey to *Madely*, was not able without a Horſe, to perform this to *Moſeley*, which was about five Miles diſtant from *Boſcobel*, and near the Mid-way from thence to *Bentley*.

It was therefore concluded, that his Majeſty ſhould ride upon *Humphrey Penderel*'s Mill-Horſe (for *Humphrey* was the Miller of *Whiteladies* Mill.) The Horſe was taken up from Graſs, and accoutred, not with rich Trappings or Furniture, befitting

F 2   ting

ting fo great a King, but with a pitiful old Saddle, and a worfe Bridle.

WHEN his Majefty was ready to take Horfe, Colonel *Carlis* humbly took Leave of him, being fo well known in the Country, that his Attendance upon his Majefty would in all Probability have proved rather a Differvice than otherwife; however, his hearty Prayers were not wanting for his Majefty's Prefervation.

THUS then his Majefty was mounted, and thus he rode towards *Mofeley*, attended by all the honeft Brothers, *William*, *John*, *Richard*, *Humphrey* and *George Penderel*, and *Francis Tates*, each of thefe took a Bill or Pike Staff on his Back, and fome of them had Piftols in their Pockets; two marched before, and one on each Side his Majefty's Horfe, and two came behind a-loof off, their Defign being this, that in Cafe they fhould have been queftioned or encountered but by five or fix Troopers, or fuch like fmall Party, they would have fhewed their Valour in defending, as well as they had done their Fidelity in otherwife ferving his Majefty: And though it was Midnight, yet they conducted his Majefty through By-ways, for better Security.

AFTER

AFTER some Experience had of the Horse, his Majesty complained, *It was the heaviest dull Jade he ever rode on;* To which *Humphrey* (the Owner of him) answered (beyond the usual Capacity of a Miller) *My Liege! Can you blame the Horse to go heavily, when he has the Weight of three Kingdoms on his Back?*

WHEN his Majesty came to *Penford* Mill, within two Miles of Mr. *Whitgreave's* House, his Guides desired him to alight and go on Foot the rest of the Way, for more Security, the Foot-Way being the more secure, and the nearer; and at last they arrived at the Place appointed by Mr. *Huddleston* (which was a little Grove of Trees in a Close of Mr. *Whitgreave's* called the *Pit-Leasow*) in order to his Majesty's being privately conveyed into Mr. *Whitgreave's* House; *William, Humphrey* and *George,* returned with the Horse, the other three attended his Majesty to the House; but his Majesty, being gone a little Way, had forgot (it seems) to bid Farewel to *William* and the rest, who were going back, so he called to them and said, *My Troubles make me forget my self! I thank you all;* and gave them his Hand to kiss.

THE

THE Lord *Wilmot,* in Purfuance of his own Appointment, came to the Meeting-Place precifely at this Hour; where Mr. *Whitgreave* received him and conveyed him to his old Chamber; but hearing nothing of the King at his prefixed Time, gave Occafion to fufpect fome Misfortune might have befal'n him, tho' the Night was very dark and rainy, which might poffibly be the Occafion of fo long Stay; Mr. *Whitgreave* therefore leaves my Lord in his Chamber, and goes to *Pit-Leafow,* where Mr. *Huddlefton* attended his Majefty's coming, and about two Hours after the Time appointed his Majefty came, whom Mr. *Whitgreave* and Mr. *Huddlefton* conveyed, with much Satisfaction, into the Houfe to my Lord, who expected him with great Solicitude, and prefently kneeled down and embraced his Majefty's Knees, who kiffed my Lord on the Cheek, and asked him earneftly, *What is become of* Buckingham, Cleveland, *and others?* To which my Lord could give little Satisfaction, but hoped they were in Safety.

My Lord foon after (addreffing himfelf to Mr *Whitgreave* and Mr. *Huddlefton*) faid, *Though I have concealed my Friend's Name all this while, now I muft tell you,*

this

this is my Master, your Master, and the Master of us all; not knowing that they understood it was the King; whereupon his Majesty was. pleased to give his Hand to Mr. *Whitgreave* and Mr. *Huddlefton* to kiss, and told them, he had received such an Account from my Lord *Wilmot* of their Fidelity, that he should never forget it; and presently asked Mr. *Whitgreave, Where is your secret Place?* Which being shewed his Majesty, he was well pleased therewith, and returning into my Lord's Chamber, sate down on the Bed-side, where his Nose fell a Bleeding; and then pulled out of his Pocket a Handkerchief, suitable to the rest of his Apparel, both coarse and dirty.

His Majesty's Attire, as was before observed in Part, was then a Leathern-Doublet, with Pewter Buttons, a Pair of old green Breeches and a Jump-Coat (as the Country calls it) of the same Green, a Pair of his own Stockings, with the Tops cut off, because embroidered, and a Pair of Stirrup Stockings, which were lent him at *Madeley*, and a Pair of old Shoes, cut and slashed to give Ease to his Feet, an old gray greasy Hat, without a Lining, a noggen Shirt, of the coarsest Linnen; his Face and his Hands made of a reechy Complexion,

plexion, by the Help of the Walnut-Tree Leaves.

Mr. *Huddleston*, obferving the Coarfnefs of his Majefty's Shirt to dif-eafe him much and hinder his Reft, asked my Lord if the King would be pleafed to change his Shirt, which his Majefty condefcended unto, and prefently put off his coarfe Shirt, and put on a flaxen one of Mr. *Huddleston's*, who pulled off his Majefty's Shoes and Stockings, and put him on frefh Stockings, and dried his Feet, where he found fome Body had innocently, but indifcreetly applied white Paper, which, with going on Foot from the Place where his Majefty alighted to the Houfe, was rolled betwixt his Stockings and his Skin, and ferved to increafe rather than affwage the Sorenefs of his Feet.

Mr. *Whitgreave* had by this Time brought up fome Bisket and a Bottle of Sack; his Majefty eat of the one, and drank a good Glafs of the other; and, being thus refrefhed, was pleafed to fay cheerfully, *I am now ready for another March; and if it fhall pleafe God once more to place me at the Head of but eight or ten thoufand Men, of one Mind, and refolved to fight, I fhall not doubt to drive thefe Rogues out of my Kingdoms.*

It

IT was now Break of the Day on *Monday* Morning the Eighth of *September*, and his Majesty was desirous to take some Rest; to which Purpose a Pallet was carried into one of the secret Places, where his Majesty lay down, but rested not so well as his Host desired; for the Place was close and inconvenient, and durst not adventure to put him into any Bed for fear of a Surprise by the Rebels.

AFTER some Rest taken in the Hole, his Majesty got up, and was pleased to take Notice of and salute Mr. *Whitgreave*'s Mother, and (having his Place of Retreat still ready) sate between whiles in a Closet over the Porch, where he might see those that passed the Road by the House.

BEFORE the Lord *Wilmot* betook himself to his Dormitory, he conferr'd with Mr. *Whitgreave*, and advised, that himself or Mr. *Huddleston* would be always vigilant about the House, and give Notice if any Soldiers came, and (says this noble Lord) *If it should so fall out, that the Rebels have Intelligence of your harbouring any of the King's Party, and should therefore put you to any Torture for Confession, be sure you discover me first, which may haply in such Case satisfy them, and preserve the King.* This

was

was the Expreffion and Care of a loyal Subject, worthy eternal Memory.

ON *Monday* his Majefty and my Lord
refolved to difpatch *John Penderel* to Colonel *Lane* at *Bentley*, with Directions for
the Colonel to fend my Lord's Horfes for
him that Night about Midnight, and to
expect him at the ufual Place: My Lord
accordingly goes to *Bentley* again, to make
Way for his Majefty's Reception there,
purfuant to a Refolution taken up by his
Majefty to go Weftward, under the Protection of Mrs. *Jane Lane's* Pafs; it being
moft probable, that the Rebels wholly
purfued his Majefty Northwards, and
would not at all fufpect him gone into the
Weft.

THIS *Monday* after Noon, Mr. *Whit-*
greave had Notice that fome Soldiers were
in the Neighbourhood, intending to apprehend him, upon Information that he had
been at *Worcefter* Fight: The King was
then laid down upon Mr. *Huddlefton's* Bed,
but Mr. *Whitgreave* prefently fecures his
Royal Gueft in the fecret Place, and my
Lord alfo, leaves open all the Chamber
Doors, and goes boldly down to the Soldiers, affuring them as his Neighbours alfo
teftified) that he had not been from home

in

in a Fortnight then laft paft; with which
Affeveration the Soldiers were fatisfied, and
came not up Stairs at all.

In this Interval the Rebels had taken a
Cornet in *Chefhire*, who came in his Majefty's Troop to *Whiteladies*, and either by
Menaces, or fome other Way, had extorted
this Confeffion from him concerning the
King (whom thefe Blood-hounds fought
with all poffible Diligence) that he came
in Company with his Majefty to *Whiteladies*, where the Rebels had no fmall Hopes
to find him; whereupon they pofted thither without ever drawing bit, almoft kill'd
their Horfes, and brought their faint-hearted
Prifoners with them.

Being come to *Whiteladies*, on *Tuefday*,
they called for Mr. *George Giffard*, who lived in an Apartment of the Houfe, pre-
fents a Piftol to his Breaft, and bad him
confefs where the King was, or he fhould
prefently die. Mr. *Giffard* was too loyal,
and too much a Gentleman to be frighted
into any Infidelity, refolutely denies the
knowing any more, but that divers Cavaliers came thither on *Wednefday* Night, eat
up their Provifion, and departed; and that
he was as ignorant who they were, as
whence they came, or whither they went,

and

and begged, if he muſt die, that they would firſt give him Leave to ſay a few Prayers. One of theſe Villains anſwered, *If you can tell us no News of the King, you ſhall ſay no Prayers:* But his diſcreet Anſwer did ſomewhat aſſwage the Fury of their Leader. They uſed the like Threats and Violence (mingled notwithſtanding with high Promiſes of Reward) to Mrs. *Anne Andrew* (to whoſe Cuſtody ſome of the King's Clothes, when he firſt took upon him the Diſguiſe were committed) who (like a true *Virago*) faithfully ſuſtain'd the one, and loyally refuſed the other, which put the Rebels into ſuch a Fury, that they ſearched every Corner of the Houſe, broke down much of the Wainſcot, and at laſt beat the Intelligencer ſeverely, for making them loſe their Labour.

DURING this *Tueſday* in my Lord *Wilmot's* Abſence, his Majeſty was for the moſt part attended by Mr. *Huddleſton*, Mr. *Whitgreave* being much abroad in the Neighbourhood, and Mrs. *Whitgreave* below Stairs, both inquiſitive after News, and the Motions of the Soldiery, in order to the Preſervation of their Royal Gueſt. The old Gentlewoman was this Day told by a Countryman, who came to her Houſe, that

that he heard the King, upon his Retreat, had beaten his Enemies at *Warrington-Bridge*; and that there were three Kings come in to his Affistance; which Story she related to his Majefty for Divertifement, who fmiling, anfwered, *Surely they are the three Kings of* Colen *come down from Heaven, for I can imagine none elfe.*

The fame Day his Majefty out of the Clofet Window, efpied two Soldiers, who paffed by the Gate in the Road, and told Mr. *Huddlefton*, he knew one of them to be a *Highlander*, and of his own Regiment; who little thought his King and Colonel to be fo near.

And his Majefty for entertainment of the Time was pleafed to difcourfe with Mr. *Huddlefton* the Particulars of the Battle of *Worcefter* (the fame in Subftance with what is before related) and by fome Words which his Majefty let fall, it might eafily be collected that his Counfels had been too often fooner difcovered to the Rebels, than executed by his Loyal Subjects.

Mr. *Huddlefton* had under his Charge young Sir *John Prefton*, Mr. *Thomas Playn*, and Mr. *Francis Reynolds*, and on this *Tuefday* in the Morning (the better to conceal his Majefty's being in the Houfe, and

G

excufe

excuse his own, more than usual long Stay above Stairs) pretended himself to be indisposed and afraid of the Soldiers, and therefore set his Scholars at several Garret Windows, and surveyed the Roads, to watch and give Notice when they saw any Troopers coming: This Service the Youths performed very diligently all Day, and at Night when they were at Supper, Sir *John* called upon his Companions, and said (more truly than he imagined) *Come Lads, let us eat lustily, for we have been upon the Life-Guard to Day.*

THIS very Day (*September* the 19th) the Rebels at *Westminster* (in further Pursuance of their bloody Designs) set forth a Proclamation, for the Discovery and apprehending CHARLES STUART (for so their frontless Impudence usually stiled his sacred Majesty) his Adherents and Abettors, with Promise of 1000*l.* Reward to whomsoever should apprehend him (so vile a Price they set upon so inestimable a Jewel.) And besides, gave strict Command to all Officers of Port-Towns, that they should permit no Person to pass beyond Sea, without special License. *And Saul sought David every Day, but God delivered him not into his Hands.*

1 Sam. xxiii. 14.

On

ON *Tuesday* Night, between twelve and one a Clock, the Lord *Wilmot* sent Colonel *Lane* to attend his Majesty to *Bentley*, Mr. *Whitgreave* meets the Colonel at the Place appointed, and brings him to the Corner of his Orchard, where the Colonel thought fit to stay whilst Mr. *Whitgreave* goes in and acquaints the King that he was come: Whereupon his Majesty took his Leave of Mr. *Whitgreave*, saluted her and gave her many Thanks for his Entertainment, but was pleased to be more particular with Mr. *Whitgreave* and Mr. *Huddleston*, not only by giving them Thanks, but by telling them, he was very sensible of the Dangers they might incur by entertaining him, if it should chance to be discovered to the Rebels; therefore his Majesty advised them to be very careful of themselves, and gave them Direction to repair to a Merchant in *London*, who should have Order to furnish them with Monies and Means of Conveyance beyond Sea, if they thought fit.

AFTER his Majesty had vouchsafed these gracious Expressions to Mr. *Whitgreave* and Mr. *Huddleston*, they told his Majesty, all the Service they could now do him, was to pray heartily to Almighty God for his Safety and Preservation, and then kneeling

G 2   down

down, his Majesty gave them his Hand to kiss, and so went down the Stairs with them into the Orchard, where Mr. *Whitgreave* both humbly and faithfully delivered his great Charge into Colonel *Lane*'s Hands, telling the Colonel who the Person was he there presented.

The Night was both dark and cold, and his Majesty's Cloathing thin, therefore Mr. *Huddleston* humbly offered his Majesty a Cloak, which he was pleased to accept, and wore to *Bentley*, from whence Mr. *Huddleston* afterwards received it.

As soon as Mr. *Whitgreave* and Mr. *Huddleston* heard his Majesty was not only got safe to *Bentley*, but marched securely from thence, they began to reflect upon his Advice, and lest any Discovery should be made of what had been acted at *Moseley*, they both absented themselves from Home; the one went to *London*, the other to a Friend's House in *Warwickshire*, where they lived privately till such Time as they heard his Majesty was safely arrived in *France*, and that no Part of the aforesaid Transactions at *Moseley* had been discovered to the Rebels, and then returned Home.

This Mr. *Whitgreave* was descended of the ancient Family of the *Whitgreaves* of *Burton*,

Burton, in the County of *Stafford,* and was first a Cornet, afterwards Lieutenant to Captain *Thomas Giffard,* in the first War for his Majesty King CHARLES the First.

MR. *John Huddleston* was a younger Brother of the renowned Family of the House of *Hutton-John,* in the County of *Cumberland,* and was a Gentleman Voluntier in his late Majesty's Service, first under Sir *John Preston,* the Elder, till Sir *John* was rendered unserviceable by the desperate Wounds he received in that Service, and after under Col. *Ralph Pudsey* at *Newark.*

HIS Majesty being safely conveyed to *Bentley* by Colonel *Lane,* stay'd there but a short Time, took the Opportunity of Mrs. *Jane's* Pass, and rode before her to *Bristol,* the Lord *Wilmot* attending, by another Way, at a Distance. In all which Journey Mrs. *Lane* performed the Part of a most faithful and prudent Servant to his Majesty, shewing her Observance, when an Opportunity would allow it, and at other Times acting her Part in the Disguise with much Discretion.

BUT the Particulars of his Majesty's Arrival at *Bristol,* and the Houses of several Loyal Subjects, both in *Somersetshire, Dorsetshire, Wiltshire, Hampshire,* and so to

Bright-

Brightbempston in *Suffex*, where he on the 15th of *October* 1651, took Shipping, and landed fecurely in *France* the next Morning; and the feveral Accidents, Hardſhips, and Encounters, in all that Journey, muſt be the admired Subject of the Second Part of his Hiſtory.

THE very next Day after his Majeſty left *Boſcobel*, being *Monday* the eighth of *September*, two Parties of Rebels came thither, the one being Part of the County Troop, who fearched the Houfe with fome Civility; the other (Captain *Broadway's* Men) did it with more Severity, eat up their little Store of Proviſion, plunder'd the Houfe of what was portable, and one of them prefented a Piſtol to *William Penderel*, and much frighted my Dame *Joan*; yet both Parties returned as ignorant, as they came, of that Intelligence they fo greedily fought after.

THIS Danger being over, honeſt *William* began to think of making Satisfaction for the fat Mutton, and accordingly tendered Mr. *Staunton* its worth in Money; but *Staunton* underſtanding the Sheep was killed for the Relief of fome honeſt Cavaliers, who had been ſheltered at *Boſcobel*, refufed to take the Money, but wiſhed, much good it might do them. THESE

THESE *Penderels* were of honest Parentage, but mean Degree, fix Brothers born at *Hobbal Grange* in the Parish of *Tong*, and County of *Salop*; *William, John, Richard, Humphrey, Thomas,* and *George; John, Thomas* and *George,* were Soldiers in the firft War for K. CHARLES I. *Thomas* was flain at *Stow* Fight, *William,* as you have heard, was a Servant at *Boscobel, Humphrey* a Miller, and *Richard* rented Part of *Hobbal Grange.*

HIS Majefty had not been long gone from *Boscobel,* but Colonel *Carlis* fent *William Penderel* to Mr. *Humphry Ironmonger,* his old Friend at *Wolverhampton*; who not only procured him a Pafs from fome of the Rebel-Commanders in a difguifed Name to go to *London,* but furnifhed him with Money for his Journey, by Means whereof he got fafe thither, and from thence into *Holland,* where he brought the firft happy News of his Majefty's Safety to his Royal Sifter the Princefs of *Orange.*

THIS Colonel *William Carlis* was born at *Brom-hall* in *Staffordshire,* within two Miles of *Boscobel,* of good Parentage, was a Perfon of approved Valour, and engaged all along in the firft War for K. CHARLES I. of happy Memory; and fince his Death

was

was no lefs active for his Royal Son; for which, and his particular Service and Fidelity before-mention'd, his Majefty was pleas'd by Letters Patents under the Great Seal of *England* to give him, by the Name of *William Carlos* (which in *Spanish* fignifies *Charles*) a very honourable Coat of Arms, *in perpetuam rei Memoriam*, as 'tis exprefs'd in the Letters Patents.

The *Oak* is now properly call'd, *The Royal Oak of Bofcobel*, nor will it lofe that Name whilft it continues a Tree, nor that Tree a Memory, whilft we have an Inn left in *England*, fince the *Royal Oak* is now become a frequent Sign both in *London*, and all the chief Cities of this Kingdom. And fince his Majefty's happy Reftauration, that thefe Myfteries have been revealed, hundreds of People for many Miles round, have flock'd to fee the famous Boscobel, which (as you have heard) had once the Honour to be the Palace of his facred Majefty, but chiefly to behold the *Royal Oak*, which has been deprived of all its young Boughs by the numerous Vifitors of it, who keep them in Memory of his Majefty's happy Prefervation; infomuch that Mr. *Fitzherbern*, who was afterwards Proprietor, was forced in a due Seafon of

the

the Year, to crop Part of it, for its Preservation, and put himself to the Charge of fencing it about with a high Pale, the better to transmit the happy Memory of it to Posterity.

THIS *Boscobel-House* has yet been a third time fortunate; for after Sir *George Booth*'s Forces were routed in *Cheshire* in *August* 1659, the Lord *Brereton*, who was engaged with him, took Sanctuary there for some Time, and was preserved.

WHEN his Majesty was thus happily convey'd away by Colonel *Lane* and his Sister, the Rebels had an Intimation that some of the Brothers were instrumental in his Preservation; so that, besides the Temptations *Humphrey* overcame at *Shefnal*, *William Penderel* was twice questioned at *Shrewsbury* on the same Account by Captain *Fox* and one *Lluellin* a Sequestrator, and *Richard* was much threatned by a peevish Neighbour at *Whiteladies*; but neither Threats nor Temptations were able to batter the Fort of their Loyalty.

AFTER this unhappy Defeat of his Majesty's Army at *Worcester*; Good God! In what strange canting Language did the *Fanaticks* communicate their Exultations to one another; particularly in a Letter (hypocritically

pocritically pretended to be written from the Church of Chrift at *Wrexham*, and printed in the *Diurnal, Nov.* 10. 1651.) there is this malignant Expreffion, *Chrift has revealed his own Arm, and broke the Arm of the Mighty once and again, and now laftly at* Worcefter; *fo that we conclude (in Ezekiel's Phrafe) there will be found no Roller to bind the late King's Arm to hold a Sword again,* &c. And that you may know who thefe falfe Prophets were, the Letter was thus fubfcribed;

Daniel Lloyd, Mor. Lloyd, John Brown, Edw. Taylor, An. Maddokes, Dav. Maurice. Men who meafured Caufes by that Succefs, which fell out according to their evil Defires, not confidering that God intended, in his own good Time, *To eftablifh the King's Throne with Juftice,* Prov. 25.

AFTER the *King had enter-*

Dan. i. 9. *ed into the Kingdom, and returned to his own Land,* the five Brothers attended him at *White-Hall* on *Wednefday* the 13th of *June* 1660. when his Majefty was pleafed to own their faithful Service, and gracioufly difmiffed them with a Princely Reward.

AND foon after Mr. *Huddlefton* and Mr. *Whitgreave* made their humble Addreffes

to

to his Majesty, from whom they likewise received a gracious Acknowledgment of their Service and Fidelity to him at *Moseley*; and this in so high a Degree of Gratitude, and with such a condescending Frame of Spirit, not at all puff'd up with Prosperity, as cannot be parallel'd in the best of Kings.

HERE let us with all glad and thankful Hearts humbly contemplate the admirable Providence of Almighty God, who contrived such wonderful Ways, and made use of such mean Instruments for the Preservation of so great a Person. Let us delight to reflect minutely on every particular, and especially on such as most approach to Miracle; let us sum up the Number of those, who were privy to this first and principal Part of his Majesty's disguise and concealment: Mr. *Giffard*, the five *Penderels*, their Mother, and three of their Wives, Colonel *Carlos*, *Francis Yates*, and his Wife, divers of the Inhabitants of *Whiteladies* (which then held five several Families) Mr. *Woolf*, his Wife, Son, Daughter and Ma'd, Mr. *Whitgreave* and his Mother, Mr. *Huddleston*, Colonel *Lane* and his Sister; and then consider whether it were not indeed a Miracle, that so many Men, and which is far more) so many Women should faithfully conceal so

important

important and unufual a Secret; and this notwithftanding the Temptations and Promifes of Reward on the one Hand, and the Danger and Menaces of Punifhment on the other.

To which I fhall add but this one Circumftance, that it was perform'd by Perfons, for the moft Part, of that Religion which has long fuffer'd under an Imputation (laid on them by fome miftaken Zealots) of Difloyalty to their Sovereign.

AND now, as we have thus thankfully commemorated the wonderful *Prefervation* of his Majefty, what remains, but that we fhould return due Thanks and Praifes for his no lefs miraculous RESTORATION; who, after a long Series of Misfortunes, and variety of Afflictions, after he had been hunted to and fro like a *Partridge upon the Mountains*, was, in God's due Time, appointed to fit, as his Vicegerent, upon the Throne of his Anceftors; and called forth to govern his own People, when they leaft expected him. For which all the Nation, even all the three Nations, had juft Caufe to fing.

Te Deum Laudamus.

BOSCOBEL;

OR, THE

HISTORY

Of the Moſt Miraculous

PRESERVATION

OF

KING *CHARLES* II.

After the

Battle of *WORCESTER.*

September the 3d, 1651.

PART II.

LONDON: Printed in the Year MDCC.XLII.

PREFACE.

THE First Part of this Miraculous History, I long since published, having the Means to be well informed in all Circumstances relating to it; the Scene (whereon those great Actions were performed) being my native Country, and many of the Actors my particular Friends.

I did not then intend to have proceeded farther, presuming some of those worthy Persons of the West (who were the happy Instruments in this Second Part) would have given us that so much desired Supplement; the rather since the Publication of the wonderful Series of this great Work, wherein the Hand of God so

miraculously

1 Sam.
x. 24.

miraculously appeared, in Preservation of Him, *whom the Lord hath cho-sen, must needs open the Eyes, and convert the Hearts of the most Disloyal.*

But finding, in all this Time, nothing done, and the World more greedy of it, than ever young Ladies were to read the Conclusion of an amorous strange Romance, after they had left the darling Lover plunged into some dire Mis-fortune, I have thus endeavoured to compleat the History.

Chiefly encouraged hereunto, by an Express *from* Lisbon, *wherein 'tis certified, that (be-sides the Translation of the* First Part of Bos-cobel *into* French) Mr. Peter Giffard of Whiteladies *has lately made it speak* Portu-guese, *and presented it to the* Infanta, *our most excellent* Queen, *who was pleased to ac-cept it with Grace, and peruse it with Passion, intimating her* Royal Desire *to see the Parti-culars, how the Hand of Providence had led the great* Monarch *of her Heart out of the treacherous Snares of so many Rebels.*

In this, I dare not undertake to deliver so many Particulars, as in the former; for though the Time of his Majesty's *Stay in those*
Western

Western Parts was longer, yet the Places were more remote, and my Lord Wilmot *(the principal Agent) dead: But I will again confidently promise to write nothing but Truth, as near as a severe Scrutiny can inform me.*

And perhaps a less Exactness in Circumstantials will better please some, who (as I have heard) object against my former Endeavours on this Royal Subject as too minutely written, and Particulars set down of too mean a Concern, for which I have yet the Example of that renowned Historian Famian Strada *to protect me, who writing of the* Emperor Charles the Fifth, *mentions what Meat he fed on such a Day, what Cloaths he wore another Time, and gives this Reason,* That it pleases, to know every Thing that Princes do, *especially when by a Chain of Providences, whose every Link seems small and weak in its single self, so great a* Blessing will, at last, be drawn in amongst us.

De Bello Belgico.

1 Sam. xxiii. 17.

That Part of this unparalled Relation of a King, *which here I undertake to deliver, may fitly, I think, be called,* The Second Stage of the Royal Progress, *wherein, as I am sure every good Subject will be astonished to read the*

H 3 *Hardships*

Hardships and Difficulties his Majesty encountered in this long and perilous *Journey*; so will they be even overjoy'd to find him, at last (by the *Conduct* of *Heaven*) brought safe to *Paris*, where my humble *Endeavours* leave him, thus comforted by the Prophet;

Fear not, for the Hand of *Saul* shall not find Thee, and Thou shalt be King over *Israel*.

T. B.

Thomas Blount.

BOS-

BOSCOBEL;

OR, THE

HISTORY

OF

King CHARLES II[ds]

Moſt miraculous Preſervation after the Battle of

WORCESTER.

The Second Stage of the Royal Progreſs.

E that well conſiders the admirable Events particularized in the Firſt Part of this Hiſtory of his Majeſty's miraculous Preſervation, will be apt to think his evil *Genius* had almoſt rack'd its Invention to find out Hardſhips and Perils beyond human Imagination, and that his good *Angel* had been

been even tired out with contriving suitable Means for his Deliverance; yet if you please (after you have sufficiently wondered and blessed God for the Preservation you read there) proceed and admire the strange stupendous Passages you shall find here; which, when you have done with just and due Attention, I cannot doubt but your Thoughts will easily raise themselves into some holy Extasy, and growing warm with often repeating their own Reflections, break forth at last, and join your Exclamations with all the true and hearty Adorers of the divine Providence.

Psal. lxxxvi. 10.

Thou art great, O Lord, and dost wonderful Things; thou art God alone.

I shall not need, I hope, to bespeak my Readers Patience for any long Introduction; since all the Complement I intend, is humbly to kiss the Pen and Paper, which have the Honour to be Servants of this Royal Subject; and without farther Ceremony begin.

Colonel *John Lane* having (as it has been related) safely conveyed his Majesty from *Moseley* to his own House at *Bentley* in *Staffordshire*, on *Tuesday* Night, the 9th of *September* 1651, the Lord *Wilmot* was there
ready

ready to receive him, and after his Majesty
had eaten and conferred with my Lord and
the Colonel of his intended Journey towards
Bristol the very next Morning, he went to
Bed, though his Rest was not like to be
long; for at the very Break of the Day on
Wednesday Morning the Colonel called up his
Majesty and brought him up a new Suit and
Cloak, which he had provided for him, of
Country grey Cloth, as near as could be
contrived like the Holy-day Suit of a Far-
mer's Son, which was thought fittest to carry on the Disguise.   Here his Majesty quitted his leather Doublet and green Breeches,
for this new grey Suit; and forsook his former Name *Will. Jones* for that of *Will.
Jackson.*

Thus then was the Royal Journey designed the King as a Tenant's Son (a Quality far more convenient for their Intention
than that of a direct Servant) was ordered
to ride before Mrs. *Jane Lane,* as her At-
tendant, Mr. *Henry Lassels* (who was Kinsman, and had been *Cornet* to the Colonel
in the late Wars) to ride single, and Mr.
John Petre of *Horton* in *Buckinghamshire,*
and his Wife, the Colonel's Sister, who
were then accidentally at *Bentley,* being bound
homeward, to ride in the same Company;
Mr.

Mr. *Petre* and his Wife little suspecting *Will. Jackson*, their fellow Traveller, to be the Monarch of *Great Britain.*

His Majesty thus refreshed, and thus accouter'd with all Necessaries for a Journey in the designed Equipage, after he had taken Leave of my Lord *Wilmot,* and agreed on their Meeting within a few Days after at Mr. *George Norton's* House at *Leigh* near *Bristol*; the Colonel convey'd him a back Way into the Stable, where he fitted his Stirrups, and gave him some Instructions for better acting the Part of *Will. Jackson,* mounted him on a good double Gelding, and directed him to come to the Gate of the House; which he punctually performed, with his Hat under his Arm.

By this Time it was Twilight, and old Mrs. *Lane* (who knew nothing of this great Secret) would needs see her beloved Daughter take Horse, which whilst she was intending, the Colonel said to the King, *Will thou must give my Sister thy Hand*; but his Majesty (unacquainted with such little Offices) offered his Hand the contrary way, which the old Gentlewoman taking Notice of, laughed, and asked the Colonel her Son, *What a goodly Horseman her Daughter had got to ride before her?*

MR.

Mr. *Petre* and his Wife, and Mr. *Laſſels* being alſo mounted, the whole Company took their Journey (under the Protection of the King of Kings) towards *Stratford* upon *Avon* in *Warwickſhire*: And ſoon after they were gone from *Bentley*, the Lord *Wilmot*, Colonel *Lane*, and *Robert Swan* my Lord's Servant, took Horſe, with a Hawk, and Spaniels with them for a Diſguiſe, intending to go that Night to Sir *Clement Fiſher*'s Houſe at *Packington* in *Warwickſhire*; where the Colonel knew they ſhould both be as welcome as Generoſity, and as ſecure as Fidelity could make them.

When the King and his ſmall Retinue arrived near *Wotton*, within four Miles of *Stratford*, they eſpy'd a Troop of Rebels, baiting (as they conceived) almoſt a Mile before them in the very Road, which cauſed a Council to be held among them, wherein Mr. *Petre* preſided, and he would by no Means go on, for fear of loſing his Horſe, or ſome other Detriment; ſo that they wheel'd about a more indirect Way, and at *Stratford* (where they were of Neceſſity to paſs the River *Avon*) met the ſame or another Troop in a narrow Paſſage, who very fairly opened to the Right and Left, and made

made Way for the Travellers to march through them.

THAT Night (according to Defignment) Mrs. *Lane*, and her Company took up their Quarters at Mr. *Tomb's* Houfe, at *Longmarfton*, fome three Miles Weft of *Stratford*, with whom fhe was well acquainted; here *Will. Jackfon* being in the Kitchen, in Purfuance of his Difguife, and the Cook Maid bufy in providing Supper for her Mafter's Friends, fhe defired him to wind up the Jack; *Will. Jackfon* was obedient, and attempted it, but hit not the right Way, which made the Maid in fome Paffion afk, *What Countryman are you, that you know not how to wind up a Jack? Will. Jackfon* anfwered very fatisfactorily, *I am a poor Tenant's Son of Colonel* Lane *in* Staffordfhire, *we feldom have roaft Meat, but when we have, we don't make ufe of a Jack*; which in fome Meafure affwaged the Maid's Indignation.

THE fame Night my Lord, with the Colonel, arrived fafely at Sir *Clement Fifber's* Houfe at *Packington*, where they found a Welcome fuitable to the Noblenefs of his Mind, and a Security anfwerable to the Faithfulnefs of his Heart.

NEXT Morning my Lord thought fit to difpatch the Colonel to *London*, to procure,

if

if poffible, a Pafs for the King, by the Name of *William Jackfon*, to go into *France*, and to bring it himfelf or fend it (as Opportunity fhould be offered) to Mr. *Norton's* Houfe, where my Lord (as you have heard) was defigned to attend his Majefty.

On *Thurfday* Morning (11th of *Sept.*) the King, with Mrs. *Lane*, and Mr. *Laffels* rofe early, and after Mrs. *Lane* had taken leave both of Mr. *Petre* and his Wife (whofe Way lay more South) and of Mr. *Tombs* the Mafter of the Houfe, they took Horfe, and without any confiderable Accident, rode by *Camden*, and arrived that Night at an Inn in *Cirencefter* in *Gloucefterfhire*, diftant about twenty four Miles from *Longmarfton*. After Supper a good Bed was provided for Mr. *Laffels*, and a Truckle-Bed for *Will. Jackfon* in the fame Chamber; but Mr. *Laffels* after the Chamberlain had left them, laid his Majefty in the beft Bed, and himfelf in the other, and ufed the like due Obfervance, when any Opportunity would allow it.

THE next Day being *Friday*, the Royal Traveller, with his Attendants, left *Cirencefter*, and by the Way of *Sudbury* rode to and through the City of *Briftol* (wherein
I they

they had once loft their Way, till Inquiry better informed them) and arrived that Evening at Mr. *Norton's* Houfe at *Leigh,* fome three Miles from *Briftol,* and about thirty from *Cirencefter,* which was the defired End of this perillous Journey.

At this Place his Majefty ftill continued under the Notion of one of Colonel *Lane's* Tenant's Sons; and, by a prefettled Contrivance with Mrs. *Lane,* feigned himfelf fick of an Ague, under colour whereof fhe procured him the better Chamber and Accommodation without any Sufpicion, and ftill took Occafion from thence with all poffible Care and Obfervance, to fend the fick Perfon fome of the beft Meat from Mr. *Norton's* Table; and Mrs. *Norton's* Maid, *Margaret Rider* who was commanded to be his Nurfe-keeper, and believed him fick indeed) made *William* a *Carduus-Poffet,* and was very careful of him; nor was his Majefty at all known or fufpected here, either by Mr. *Norton* or his Lady, from whofe Knowledge yet, he was not concealed out of any the leaft Diftruft of their Fidelity (for his whole Dominions yielded not more faithful Subjects) but becaufe fuch Knowledge might haply at unawares have drawn a greater Refpect and Obfervance

vance from them, than that Exigent would safely admit of.

UNDER the Disguise of this Ague his Majesty for the most Part kept his Chamber, during his Stay at *Leigh*; yet, being somewhat wearied with that kind of Imprisonment, one Day (when his Ague might be imagined to be in the Intermission) he walk'd down to a Place, where the young Men played at a Game of Ball called *Fives,* where his Majesty was ask'd by one of the Gamesters, if he could play, and would take his Part at that Game; he pleaded Unskilfulness, and modestly refused.

BUT behold an unexpected Accident here fell out, which put his Majesty and Mrs. *Lane* into some Apprehension of the Danger of a Discovery. Mr. *Norton*'s Butler (whose Name was *John Pope*) had served a Courtier some Years before the War, under Colonel *Bagot* at *Litchfield,* and by that Means had the Physiognomy of the King then Prince of *Wales*) so much imprinted in his Memory, that tho' his Majesty was in all Points most accurately disguised) yet the Butler knew him, and communicated his Knowledge to Mrs *Lane,* who at first absolutely denied him to be the

King,

King, but after, upon Conference and Advice had with his Majesty, it was thought best to acknowledge it to the Butler, and, by the Bonds of Allegiance, conjure him to Secrecy, who thereupon kissed the King's Hand, and proved perfectly honest.

On *Saturday* Night (13th of *September*) the Lord *Wilmot* arrived at a Village near *Leigh* where he lay, but came every Day to visit *Will. Jackson* and Mrs. *Lane*; as Persons of his Acquaintance; and so had the Opportunity to attend and consult with his Majesty unsuspected, during their stay at *Leigh*.

Soon after, upon serious Advice had with my Lord, it was resolved by his Majesty to go to *Trent*, the House of Colonel *Francis Wyndham* (of whose Fidelity his Majesty had ample Assurance) which lies in *Somersetshire*, but bordering on the very Skirts of *Dorsetshire* near *Sherburn*; and therefore was judged to be conveniently seated in the Way towards *Lime* and other Port Towns, where his Majesty might probably take Shipping for *France*.

In Pursuance of this Resolve, the Lord *Wilmot* (as his Majesty's Harbinger) rode to *Trent* on *Monday*, to make Way for his more private Reception there; and *Tues-day*

day Morning *(Sept. 16.)* his MAJESTY's Ague being then (as was pretended) in the Recess, he repaired to the Stable, and there gave Order for making ready the Horses, and then it was signified from Mrs. *Lane,* (tho' before so agreed) that *William Jackson* should ride single and carry the Portmanteau; accordingly they mounted, being attended Part of the Way by one of Mr. *Norton's* Men as a Guide, and that Day rode through the Body of *Somerset-shire,* to Mr. *Edward Kirton's* House at *Castle-Cary,* near *Burton,* where his Majesty lay that Night, and next Morning arrived at Colonel *Wyndham's* said House, which was about twenty six Miles from *Leigh.*

His Majesty was now at *Trent,* in as much Safety, as the Master of the House his Fidelity and Prudence could make him; but the great Work was how to procure a Vessel for Transportation of this great Treasure; for this End his Majesty, the Lord *Wilmot,* Colonel *Wyndham,* had several Consults, and in Pursuance of their Determination, the Colonel with his trusty Servant *Henry Peters,* posted to *Lime,* which is about twenty Miles from *Trent,* where, after some Difficulty, by the Assi-

I 3   stance

stance of Captain *William Elsden*, a loyal Subject (at whose House the Colonel lodged) he hir'd a Bark to transport his Majesty for *France*, which Bark was by Agreement to attend at *Charmouth* (a little maritime near *Lime*) at a Time appointed, and return'd with all speed to *Trent* with the good News.

THE next Day his Majesty resolved for *Lime*, and Mrs. *Jane Lane* here humbly took her Leave of him, returning with Mr. *Lassels*, by his Majesty's Permission into *Staffordshire*, leaving him in faithful Hands, and in a hopeful Way of escaping the bloody Designs of merciless Rebels; which as it was all along the Scope of her Endeavours, so was it now the Subject of her Prayers; yet it was still thought the best Disguise, for his Majesty to ride before some Woman; and accordingly Mrs. *Julian Conningsby*, Colonel *Wyndham*'s Kinswoman, had the Honour to ride behind his Majesty; who with the Lord *Wilmot*, the Colonel, and *Henry Peters*, came that Evening to a blind Inn in *Charmouth*, near which Place the Skipper had promised to be in readiness with his Bark; but observe the Disappointment.

IN the Interim (whilst Colonel *Wyndham* was gone back to *Trent*) it seems the *Rebels Proclamation*, for apprehending CHARLES STUART (meaning in their impudent Phrase) our then gracious King, and prohibiting, for a certain Time, the Transportation of any Person without a particular License, had been published in and about *Lime*, and the Skipper having acquainted his Wife, that he had agreed to transport two or three Persons into *France*, whom he believed might be Cavaliers, it seems the *Grey Mare* was the *better Horse* ; for she locked up her Husband in his Chamber, and would by no Means permit him to go the Voyage ; so that whilst *Henry Peters* stay'd on the Beach most Part of the Night ; his Majesty, and the rest of the Company sate up in the Inn, expecting News of the Seaman with his Boat who never appeared.

THE next Morning his Majesty and Attendants resolving to return to *Trent*, rode first to *Bridport* in *Dorsetshire*, where he stay'd at an Inn, whilst *Henry Peters* was sent back to Captain *Elsden*, to see if there were any Hope left of persuading the Skipper, or rather of gaining Leave of his Wife, for him to undertake the Voyage ; but

but all Endeavours proved ineffectual, and by that Time *Harry* returned, the Day was so far spent, that his Majesty could conveniently reach no farther that Night than *Broad-Windsor*; and (which added much to the Danger) Col. *Heane* (one of *Cromwell's* Commanders) at this very Time was marching Rebels from several Garrisons to *Weymouth*, and other adjacent Ports, in order to their being shipped, for the forcing the Island of *Jersey* from his Majesty's Obedience, as they had done all the rest of his Dominions; so that the Roads of this Country were full of Soldiers.

Broad-Windsor afforded but one Inn, and that the *George*, a mean one two (and which was worse) the best Accommodations in it were, before his Majesty's Arrival, taken up by Rebel Soldiers, one of whose Doxies was brought to Bed in the House, which caused the Constable and Overseers for the Poor of the Parish to come thither at an unseasonable Hour of the Night, to take Care that the Brat might not be left to the Charge of the Parish; so that his Majesty, through this Disturbance went not to Bed at all, and we may safely conclude, he took as little rest

rest here, as he did the Night before at *Charmouth.* Thus were *the Tribulation of David's Heart enlarged,* and he prayed, *Deliver me, O Lord, from my Distresses.*

His Majesty having still thus miraculously escaped Dangers, which hourly environed him, returned safe to *Trent* next Morning, where, after some Refreshment and Rest taken, he was pleased to call my Lord *Wilmot* and Colonel *Wyndham* (the Members of his little Privy Council) together, to consider what Way was next to be attempted for his Transportation.

After several Proposals, it was at last resolved that my Lord (attended and conducted by *Henry Peters*) should the next Day be sent to *Salisbury,* to Mr. *John Coventry* (Son to the late Lord *Coventry,* Lord Keeper of the Great Seal of *England*) who then lived in the *Close* of that City, and was known to be both a prudent Person and a perfect Lover of his Sovereign, as well to advise how to procure a Bark for passing his Majesty into *France,* as for providing some Monies for his present necessary Occasions.

My Lord being arrived at *Salisbury,* dispatched *Henry Peters* back to *Trent,* with Intimation of the good Reception he
found

found there; for, Mr. *Coventry* did not only furnish him with Monies, but was very solicitous for his Majesty's Safety; to which End he advised with Dr. *Humphrey Henchman*, a worthy Divine, who since his Majesty's happy Restauration, was with much Merit advanced to the Episcopal See of *Salisbury*.

THE Result of these two loyal Persons Consultation was, that his Majesty should be desired to remove to *Hele* (which lay about three Miles North-East of *Salisbury*) the Dwelling-House of Mrs. *Mary Hyde*, the Relict of *Laurence Hyde*, Esq; eldest Brother to honourable Sir *Robert Hyde*, one of the Justices of his Majesty's Court of *Common-Pleas*, whom they knew to be both as discreet and as loyal, as any of her Sex.

WITH this Resolution and Advice Mr. *Coventry* dispatched his Chaplain, Mr. *John Selleck* to *Trent* with a Letter, rolled up into the Bigness of Musket Bullet, which the faithful Messenger had Order to swallow down his Throat, in Case of any Danger.

MEAN Time Mr. *Coventry* had found out a trusty Seaman at *Southampton*, who undertook to transport whom he pleased; but on second Thoughts and Advice had

with

with my Lord *Wilmot*, it was not held safe for his Majesty to take Shipping there, in regard of the so many Castles by which the Ships pass, that are outward bound, and the often Examination of the Passengers in them; so that some of the small Ports of *Suffex* were concluded to be the safer Places for effecting this great Work of his Majesty's Delivery from the Hands of such unparallel'd Rebels, who even ravenously thirsted after Royal Blood.

IN the Interim Mr. *Selleck* returned with his Majesty's Resolution to come to *Hole*, signified by a like paper Bullet; and by this Time his Majesty thought fit to admit of the Service and Assistance of Colonel *Robert Philips* (Grandson to the famous Sir *Edward Philips*, late Master of the Rolls) who lived in those Parts, and was well acquainted with the Ways of the Country, and known to be as faithful as Loyalty could make him: This Colonel undertook to be his Majesty's Conductor to *Hole*, which was near thirty Miles distant from *Trent*.

DURING his Majesty's Stay at *Trent* (which was about a Fortnight) he was, for his own Security, forced to confine himself to the voluntary Imprisonment of his Chamber,

Chamber, which was happily accommodated (in cafe the Rebels had fearched the Houfe) with an old well-contrived fecret Place, long before made (for a Shelter against the Inquifition of Purfuivants) by fome of the ancient Family of the *Gerbards*, Col. *Wyndham's* Lady's Anceftors, who were *Recufants*, and had formerly been Owners of that Houfe.

His Majefty's Meat was likewife (to prevent the Danger of a Difcovery) for the moft Part dreffed in his own Chamber, the Cookery whereof ferved him for fome Divertifement of the Time: And it is a great Truth if we fay, there was no Coft fpared, nor Care wanting in the Colonel, for the Entertainment and Prefervation of his Royal Gueft.

On the 3d of *October*, his Majefty (having given Colonel *Wyndham* particular Thanks for his great Care and Fidelity towards him) left *Trent*, and began his Journey with Colonel *Philips*, and perfonating a Tenant's Son of his, towards *Hele*, attended by *Henry Peters* (afterwards Yeoman of the Field to his Majefty) and riding before Mr. *Conningsby.* The Travellers paffed by *Wincanton*, and near the midft of that Day's Journey, arrived at *Mere*, a

little

little Market Town in *Wiltshire*, and dined at the *George* Inn; the Host, Mr. *Christopher Philips*, whom the Colonel knew to be perfectly honest.

THE Host sate at the Table with his Majesty, and administred Matters of Discourse, told the Colonel, for News, that he heard the Men of *Westminster* (meaning the Rebels) notwithstanding their Victory at *Worcester*, were in a great Maze, not knowing what was become of the King; but (says he) it is the most received Opinion that he is come in a Disguise to *London*, and many Houses have been searched for him there; at which his Majesty was observed to smile.

AFTER Dinner mine Host familiarly asked the King, *if he were a Friend to* Cæsar? To which his Majesty answered, *Yes;* Then said he, *Here's a Health to King* CHARLES, in a Glass of Wine, which his Majesty and the Colonel both pledged; and that Evening arrived in Safety at *Hele.* And his Majesty since his happy Return has been pleased to ask, *What was become of his honest Host at* Mere?

IN the mean Time the Lord *Wilmot* (who took up the borrowed Name of Mr. *Barlow*) rode to such Gentlemen of his

K

Acquain-

Acquaintance in *Hampshire,* whom he knew
to be faithful Sujects, to seek Means for
(what he so much desired) the Transportation of his Majesty; and first repaired to
Mr. *Laurence Hyde* (a Name as faithful as
fortunate in his Majesty's Service at his
House at *Hinton D'aubigny* near *Catharing-
ton,* then to Mr. *Thomas Henslow* at *Bur-
hant,* in the same County) to whom (as
Persons of known Fidelity) my Lord communicated his weighty Business, and desired
their Assistance for procuring a Bark for his
Majesty's Transportation.

Mr. *Henslow* (in Zeal to this Service)
immediately acquainted the Earl of *Southampton* (then at his House at *Titchfield,*
and afterwards with much Merit dignified
with the great Office of *Lord High Trea-
surer of* England) with this most important Affair; my Lord *Wilmot* judging it
fitter for Mr. *Henslow* (his Neighbour) to
do it, than for himself, in those Circumstances, to appear at my Lord's House;
whose eminent Fidelity and singular Prudence, in the Conduct of even the greatest Affairs of State, being known both to
them and all the World, and his great
Power and Command at *Bewly* Haven, and
the Maritime Parts of *Hampshire,* esteemed
very

very favourable for their Defign, wherein his Lordſhip was extreamly active and ſolicitous.

Besides this, Mr. *Laurence Hyde* recommended my Lord *Wilmot* to Colonel *George Gunter*, who lived at *Rackton* near *Chicheſter* in *Suſſex*; and was known to be both faithful and active, not unlike to be ſucceſsful in this Service, to whom therefore my Lord haſted, and lay at *Rackton* one Night, where he imparted his great Solicitation to the Colonel, and his Kinſman Mr. *Thomas Gunter*, who was then accidentally there.

All theſe Perſons had the like Inſtructions from my Lord, which made a deep Impreſſion on their loyal Hearts, and excited them to uſe their utmoſt Endeavours by ſeveral Ways and Means to procure the *Noah's Ark*, which might at laſt ſecure his Majeſty from the great Inundation of Rebellion and Treaſon, which then did overſpread the Face of his whole Dominions.

But to return to my humble Obſervance of his Majeſty at *Hele*, where Mrs. *Hyde* was ſo tranſported with Joy and Loyalty towards him, that at Supper, though his Majeſty was ſet at the lower End of the Table, yet the good Gentlewoman had

K 2   much

much ado to overcome herfelf, and not to carve to him firft; however fhe could not refrain from drinking to him in a Glafs of Wine, and giving him two Larks, when others had but one.

AFTER Supper Mr. *Frederick Hyde* (Brother-in-Law to the Widow, who was then at *Hele*, and fince created *Serjeant at Law*) difcourfed with his Majefty upon various Subjects, not fufpecting who he was, but wondered to receive fuch rational Difcourfe from a Perfon, whofe Habit fpoke him but of mean Degree; and when his Majefty was brought to his Chamber, Dr. *Henchman* attended him there, and had a long and private Communication with him.

NEXT Day it was thought fit, to prevent the Danger of any Difcovery, or even Sufpicion in the Houfe, that in regard his Majefty might poffibly ftay there fome Days before the Conveniency of a Tranfportation could be found out, he fhould that Day publickly take his Leave, and ride about two Miles from the Houfe, and then be privately brought in again the fame Evening, when all the Servants were at Supper; which was accordingly performed, and after that Time his Majefty appeared no more at *Hele* in Publick, but had

Meat

Meat brought him privately to his Chamber, and was attended by the good Widow with much Care and Observance.

Now among the many faithful Solicitors for this long expected Bark, Colonel *Gunter* happened to be the lucky Man, who first procured it at *Brighthemston* in *Sussex*, by the Affistance of Mr. *Francis Manfel*, Merchant of *Chichester*; and the concurrent Endeavours of Mr. *Thomas Gunter*: And on *Saturday* Night the eleventh of *October*, he brought the happy Tidings to my Lord *Wilmot*, and Colonel *Philips*, who then lay; the one at Mr. *Laurence Hyde's*, the other at Mr. *Anthony Brown's* House, his Neighbour and Tenant.

The next Morning, being *Sunday*, Colonel *Philips* was difpatch'd to *Hele* with the much defired News, and with Inftructions to attend his Majesty on *Monday* to the *Downs*, called *Old Winchefter*, near *Warnford*.

Early in the Morning his Majesty was privately conveyed from *Hele*, and went on Foot at leaft two Miles to *Charendon* Park Corner, attended by Dr. *Henchman*; then took Horfe with Colonel *Phillips*; and at the appointed Time and Place the Lord *Wilmot*, Col. *Gunter*, and Mr. *Thomas Gun-*

K 3 *ter*

ter met his Majefty, with a Brace of Grey-hounds, the better to carry on the Difguife.

THAT Night, though both Mr. *Laurence Hyde* and Mr. *Henflow* had each of them provided a fecure Lodging for his Majefty, by the Lord *Wilmot's* Order, yet it was judged fitteft by Colonel *Gunter*, and accordingly agreed unto by my Lord, that his Majefty fhould lodge at Mr. *Thomas Symon's* Houfe at *Hamblkden* in *Hampfhire*, who married the Colonels Sifter, in regard the Colonel knew them to be very faithful, but chiefly becaufe it lay more directly in the Way from *Hele* to *Brighthemfton*; and accordingly Colonel *Gunter* attended his Majefty to his Sifter's Houfe that Night, who provided a good Supper for them, though fhe had not the leaft Sufpicion or Intimation of his Majefty's Prefence among them.

THE King and his fmall Retinue arriving in Safety at Mrs. *Symon's* Houfe on *Monday* Night the 13th of *October*, were heartily welcomed by Mrs. *Symens*, for her Hufband was not then at Home; but by that Time they had fupp'd in comes Mr *Symons*, who wondering to fee fo many Strangers in his Houfe, was affured by his Brother

ther *Gunter*, that they were all honest Gentlemen; yet, at first Interview, he much suspected Mr *Jackson* to be a *Round-head*, observing how little Hair *William Penderel*'s Scissers had left him; but at last being satisfied they were all Cavaliers, he soon laid open his Heart, and thought nothing too good for them, was sorry his Beer was no stronger, and, to encourage it, fetch'd down a Bottle of Strong-Water, and, mixing it with the Beer, drank a cheerful Cup to Mr. *Jackson*, calling him *Brother Round-head*, whom his Majesty pledged; who was here observed to be cloathed in a short *Juppa* of a sad coloured Cloth, and his Breeches of another Species, with a black Hat, and without Cuffs, somewhat like the meaner Sort of Country Gentlemen.

Mr. *Symons*, in the Time of entertaining his Guests, did by chance let fall an Oath, for which Mr. *Jackson* took Occasion modestly to reprove him.

His Majesty, thus resting himself *Monday* Night at *Hambledon*, early on *Tuesday* Morning (*October* the 14th) prepared for his Journey to *Brighthemston*, distant about thirty five Miles from thence: But (having then no further use for Colonel *Philips*) dismissed miffed him with Thanks for his Fidelity and Service, in this most secret and important Affair; and then, having also bidden Farewell to Mr. *Symons* and his Wife, took Horse, attended by my Lord *Wilmot* and his Man, Colonel *Gunter*, and Mr. *Thomas Gunter.*

WHEN they came near the Lord *Lumley's* House at *Stanstead* in *Suffex*, it was considered, that the Greatness of the Number of Horse might possibly raise some Suspicion of them, Mr. *Thomas Gunter* was therefore dismissed with Thanks, for the Service he had done, and his Majesty held on his Journey without any Stay; and being come to *Bramber* within seven Miles of the desired Port, met there some of Colonel *Herbert Morley's* Soldiers, who yet did neither examine, nor had they, as far as could be discerned, the least Suspicion of the Royal Passengers, who arrived at last at the *George* Inn in *Brightbemston*, where Mr. *Francis Mansel*, who assisted Colonel *Gunter* in this happy Service, had agreed to meet him.

AT Supper Mr. *Mansel* sate at the upper End of the Table, and Mr. *Jackson* (for that Name his Majesty still retained) at the lower End. The Inn-Keeper's Name was

was *Smith*, and had formerly related to the Court, so that he suspected Mr. *Jackson* to be whom he really was, which his Majesty understanding, he discoursed with his Host after Supper, whereby his Loyalty was confirmed; and the Man proved faithful.

THE next Morning, being *Wednesday October* the 15th (the same Day on which the noble Earl of *Derby* became a Royal *Martyr* at *Boult n*) his Majesty, having given particular Thanks to Colonel *Gunter*, for his great Care, Pains and Fidelity towards him, took Shipping with the Lord *Wilmot* in the Bark, which lay in Readiness for him at that Harbour, and whereof Mr. *Nicholas Tetersal* was Owner; and the next Day, with an auspicious Gale of Wind, landed safe at *Fecam* near *Havre de Grace* in *Normandy*; where his Majesty might happily say with *David, Thou hast delivered me from the violent Man; therefore will I sing Praises to thy Name, O Lord.*

THIS very Bark, after his Majesty's Restauration, was by Captain *Tetersal* brought into the River *Thames*, and lay some Months at Anchor before *Whitehall*, to renew

new the Memory of the happy Service it had performed.

His Majesty having nobly rewarded Captain *Titersal*, in Gold, for his Transportation, lodged this Night at an Inn in *Fecam*, and the next Day rode to *Roan*, still attended by the faithful Lord *Wilmot*, where he continued *Incognito* several Days at Mr. *Scot*'s House, since created *Baronet*, till he had sent an Express to the Queen, his Royal Mother, who had been long solicitous to hear of his Safety, and the Court of *France*, intimating his safe Arrival there, and had quitted his disguised Habit for one more befitting the Dignity of so great a KING.

Upon the first Intelligence of this welcome News, his Highness, the Duke of *York* sent his Coach forthwith to attend his Majesty at *Roan*, and the Lord *Gerard*, with others his Majesty's Servants, made all possible Haste, with glad Hearts, to perform their Duty to him. So that on the 29th of *October*, his Majesty set forward towards *Paris*, lay that Night at *Fleury*, about seven Leagues from *Roan*; the next Morning his Royal Brother, the Duke of *York*, was ready to receive him at *Magnie*, and that Evening his Majesty was met

met at *Monçeaux*, a Village near *Paris*, by the Queen of *England*, accompanied with her Brother, the Duke of *Orleans*, and attended by a great Number of Coaches, and many both *English* and *French* Lords and Gentlemen on Horfeback, and was thus gladly conducted the fame Night, though fomewhat late, to the *Louvre* at *Paris*, to the inexpreffible Joy of his dear Mother, the Queen, his Royal Brother the Duke of *York*, and of all true Hearts.

HERE we muft again, with greater Reafon, humbly contemplate the admirable Providence of Almighty God, which certainly never appeared more miraculoufly than in this ftrange Deliverance of his Majefty from fuch an Infinity of Dangers, that Hiftory it felf cannot produce a Parallel, nor will Pofterity willingly believe it.

FROM the 3d of *September* at *Worcefter* to the 15th of *October* at *Brighthemfton*, being one and forty Days, he paffed through more Dangers than he travelled Miles, of which yet he traverfed in that Time only near three hundred (not to fpeak of his Dangers at Sea, both at his coming into *Scotland*, and his going out of *England*, nor of his long March from

Scotland

cotland to *Worcester*) fometimes on Foot with uneafy Shoes; at other Times on Horfeback, encumbered with a Portmanteau, and which was worfe, at another Time on the gall-back'd, flow-pac'd Miller's Horfe; fometime acting one Difguife in coarfe Linnen and a leather Doublet; fometimes another, of almoft as bad a Complection; one Day he is forced to fculk in a Barn at *Madeley*; another Day fits with Colonel *Carlos* in a Tree, with his Feet extreamly gall'd, and at Night glad to lodge with *William Penderel* in a fecret Place at *Bofcobel*, which never was intended for the Dormitory of a King.

SOMETIMES he was forced to fhift with coarfe Fare for a Belly-full; another Time in a Wood, glad to receive the Neceffities of Nature with a Mefs of Milk, ferved up in an homely Difh by Good-Wife *Yates*, a poor Country Woman; then again, for a Variety of Tribulation, when he thought himfelf almoft out of Danger, he directly meets fome of thofe Rebels, who fo greedily fought his Blood, yet, by God's great Providence, had not the Power to difcover him; and (which is more than has yet been mentioned) he fent at another Time to fome Subjects for Relief and Affiftance

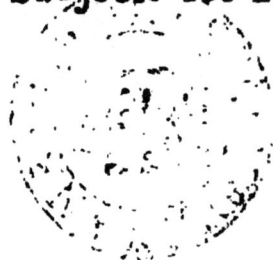

in

in his great Neceſſity, who out of a puſilla-
nimous Fear of the bloody *Arch-Rebel,* then
reigning, durſt not own him.

BESIDES all this 'twas not the leaſt of his
Afflictions daily to hear the Earl of *Derby,*
and other his loyal Subjects, ſome murdered,
ſome impriſoned, and others ſequeſtred in
Heaps, by the ſame *bloody Uſurper,* only for
performing their Duty to their lawful KING.
In a Word, there was no Kind of Miſery
(but Death it ſelf of which his Majeſty, in
this horrid Perſecution, did not in ſome
Meaſure, both in Body, Mind and Eſtate,
bear a very great Share; yet ſuch was his
invincible *Patience* in this Time of Trial,
ſuch his *Fortitude,* that he overcame them all
with ſuch pious Advantage to himſelf, that
their Memory is now ſweet, and *it was good
for him, that he had been afflicted.*

OF theſe his Majeſty's Sufferings and forced Extermination from his own Dominions,
England's * *Great Chancellor* thus excellently
deſcants.

---

* Edward *Earl of* Clarendon. *See* p. 291, *of the*
Appendix *to his Lordſhip's* Hiſtory *of the* Grand Rebellion.

L   WE

WE may tell those desperate Wretches, who yet harbour in their Thought, wicked Designs against the sacred Person of the King, in order to the compassing their own Imaginations, that God Almighty would not have led him through so many Wildernesses of Afflictions of all Kinds, conducted him through so many Perils by Sea, and Perils by Land, snatch'd him out of the midst of this Kingdom, when it was not worthy of him, and when the Hands of his Enemies were even upon him, when they thought themselves so sure of him, that they would bid so cheap and so vile a Price for him: He would not in that Article have so covered him with a Cloud, that he travelled even with some Pleasure and great Observation through the midst of his Enemies: He would not so wonderfully have new modelled that Army; so inspired their Hearts and the Hearts of the whole Nation with an honest and impatient Longing for the Return of their dear Sovereign, and in the mean Time have exercised him (which had little less of Providence in it than the other) with those unnatural, or at least unusual Dis-respects, and Reproaches abroad, that he might have a harmless and an innocent Appetite to his own Country, and return to his own People, with a full Value, and the whole

unwasted

unwasted Bulk of his Affections, without being corrupted or byassed by extraordinary foreign Obligations: God Almighty would not have done all this but for a Servant, whom he will always preserve, as the Apple of his own Eye, and always defend the most secret Michinations of his Enemies.

THUS the best and happiest of Orators.

SOME may haply here expect I should have continued the particulars of this History to the Time of his Majesty's happy Restauration, by giving an Account of the Reception his Majesty found from the several Princes beyond the Seas, during his Exile, and of his Evenness of Mind, and prudent Deportment towards them, upon all Occasions; but that was clearly beyond the Scope of my Intention, which aimed only to write the *Wonderful History* of a great and good King, violently pursued in his own Dominions by the worst of *Rebels,* and miraculously preserved, under God, by the best of Subjects.

IN other Countries, of which his Majesty traversed not a few, he found Kindness and a just Compassion of his Adversity from many, and from some a Neglect and Dis-regard;

gard; yet, in all the almoſt nine Years A-
broad, I have not heard of any Paſſage that
approached the Degree of a Miracle like
that at Home; therefore I may, with Faith
to my own Intentions, not improperly make
a ſilent Tranſition from his Majeſty's Arri-
ral at *Paris*, on the thirtieth Day of *October*,
1651, to his Return to *London* on the nine
and twentieth of *May*, 1660; and with a
Te Deum Laudamus, ſum up all, and ſay
with the Prophet;

2 Sam.   *My Lord, the King, is come a-*
xix. 30. *gain in Peace, to his own Houſe.*

1 Sam.   *And all the People ſhouted, and*
xx. 24. *ſaid,* GOD SAVE THE KING.

F I N I S.

Clauſtrum Regale Reſeratum:

OR,

KING *CHARLES* IId's

CONCEALMENT

AT

TREN T.

Publiſhed by Mrs. ANN WYNDHAM.

In umbra alarum tuarum ſperabo, donec tranſeat iniquitas.

LONDON:

Printed in the YEAR M,DCC,XLIII.

TO THE

QUEEN's

MOST EXCELLENT

MAJESTY.

*T*HIS little Book having obtained Liberty, after a long Imprisonment, to walk Abroad, prostrates it self at Your Majesty's Feet for Patronage and Protection. In it your Majesty may behold GOD's wonderful Mercy and Providence, in keeping and preserving our Gracious Sovereign from the Hands of his Enemies, when they so pleased themselves with the Hopes of seizing His Sacred Person after the

Battle

Battle of Worcester; as they had invented and prepared new Ways to afflict His Majesty, such as, till then, never entred into the Hearts of the worst of Tyrants before them. But it pleased God to frustrate the Hopes and Designs of the King's Adversaries, and to restore His Majesty to His Father's Throne: Which that he may long enjoy with Your Majesty, in Health, Peace and Happiness, is, and shall be, the Prayer of

Your MAJESTY's,

Most obedient, and

Most faithful Servant,

ANNE WYNDHAM.

Clauſtrum Regale Reſèratum:

OR, THE

KING'S CONCEALMENT

AT

TRENT.

N O W that after the Battle of *Worceſter*, his Sacred Majeſty moſt wonderfully eſcaped the Hands of his Blood-thirſty Enemies, and (under a Diſguiſe, in the Company of Mrs. *Jane Lane*) ſafely arrived at *Abbots-Leigh* in *Somerſetſhire* (the Seat of Sir *George Norton*, lying near to the City of *Briſtol*) hath been fully publiſhed unto the World. His Majeſty's Journey from thence to the Houſe of Colonel *Francis Wyndham* at *Trent*, in the ſame County, his Stay there, his Endeavour (though fruſtrate) to get over

into

into *France*, his Return to *Trent*, his final
Departure thence in order to his happy
Tranfportation, are the Subject of this prefent Relation.   A Story, in which the Con-
ftellation of Providence are fo refulgent, that
their Light is fufficient to confute all the A-
theifts of the World, and to enforce all Perfons (whofe Faculties are not pertinacioufly
deprav'd) to acknowledge a watchful Eye of
GOD from above, looking upon all Actions
of Men here below, making even the moft
Wicked fubfervient to his juft and glorious
Defigns.   And indeed, whatfoever the An-
cients fabled of *Gyge*'s Ring, by which he
could render himfelf invifible, or the Poets
fancied of their Gods, who ufually carried
their chief Favourites in the Clouds, and by
drawing thofe aerial Curtains, did fo conceal
them, that they were heard and feen of
none, whilft they both heard and faw others,
is here moft certainly verified.   For, the
Almighty fo clofely covered the King, with
the Wing of his Protection, and fo clouded
the Underftanding of his cruel Enemies,
that the moft piercing Eye of Malice could
not fee, nor the moft barbaroufly-bloody
Hand offer Violence to his facred Perfon;
God fmiting his Purfuers (as once he did the
Sodomites) with Blindnefs, who with as much
Eagernefs

Eagerness fought to facrifice the Lord's A-
nointed to their Fury, as the other did to
proſtitute the Angels to their Luſts.

But before the ſeveral Particulars of this
Story are laid open, two Queſtions (eaſily
foreſeen) which will be readily aſked by every Reader, call for an Anſwer. The one is,
Why this Relation, ſo much expected, ſo
much longed for, has been kept up all this
while from publick View? And the other,
How it comes to paſs, that it now takes the
Liberty to walk abroad? Concerning the
firſt, it muſt be known, that a Narrative of
theſe Paſſages was (by eſpecial Command
from his Majeſty) written by the Colonel's
own Hand, immediately after the King's
Return into *England*; which (being preſen-
ted to his Majeſty) was laid up in his Royal
Cabinet, there to reſt for ſome Time, it being the King's Pleaſure (for Reaſons beſt
known to his ſacred Self) that it ſhould not
be then publiſhed.

And as his Majeſty's Command to keep
it private, is a ſatisfactory Anſwer to the
firſt; ſo, his Licence now obtained that it
might travel abroad, may ſufficiently reſolve
the ſecond Queſtion. But beſides this, many prevalent Reaſons there are, which plead
for a Publication; the chief of which are
theſe;

these : That the implacable Enemies of this Crown may be for ever silenced and ashamed ; who having neither Law nor Religion to patronize their unjust Undertakings, construed a bare Permission, to be a divine Approbation of their Actions; and (taking the Almighty to be such a one as themselves) blasphemously entitled God to be the Author of all their Wickedness. But the Arm of God stretched out from Heaven to the Rescue of the King, cutting off the Clue of their Success, even then when they thought they had spun up their Thread, hath not left them so much as an Apron of Fig-Leaves to cover the Nakedness of their most shameful Proceedings.

The next is, That the Truth of his Majesty's Escape (being minced by some, mistaken by others, and not fully set forth by any) might appear in its native Beauty and Splendor; that as every Dust of Gold is Gold, and every Ray of Light is Light, so every Jot and Tittle of Truth being Truth, not one Grain of the Treasure, nor one Beam of the Lustre of this Story might be lost or clouded; it being so rare, so excellent, that aged Time out of all the Archives of Antiquity can hardly produce a Parallel. Singularly admirable indeed it is, if we consider

sider

fider the Circumſtances and Actors. The Colonel (who chiefly deſigned, and moved in this great Affair) could not have had the Freedom to have ſerved his Majeſty, had he not been a Priſoner; his very Confinement giving him both a Liberty and Protection to act For, coming Home from *Weymouth*, upon his Parole, he had the Opportunity to travel freely, without fear of being ſtopped, and taken up: And being newly removed from *Sherbone* to *Trent*, the jealous Eye of *Somerſetſhire* Potentates had ſcarce then found out, whoſe male-volent Aſpect afterwards ſeldom ſuffered him to live at Home, and too too often furniſhed his Houſe with very unwelcome Gueſts. Others, who contributed their Aſſiſtance, were Perſons of both Sexes, and of very different Conditions and Qualities: And although their Endeavours often proved ſucceſsleſs, though they had received Diſcouragements on one Hand, were terrified with Threats on the other; that a Seal of Silence ſhould be imprinted upon the Lips of Women, who are become proverbial for their Garrulity; that Faithfulneſs and Conſtancy ſhould guard the Hearts of Servants, who are uſually corrupted with Rewards, or affrighted with Puniſhments; that neither

M   Hope

Hope nor Fear (moſt powerful Paſſions, heightened by capital Animadverſions proclaimed againſt all that ſhould conceal, and large Remunerations promiſed to ſuch as ſhould diſcover the King) could work nothing upon any ſingle Perſon, ſo as to remove him or her from their reſpective Duty, but that all ſhould harmoniouſly concenter, both in the Deſign, and alſo afterward keep them ſo long cloſe ſhut up under the Lock of Secrecy, that nothing could be diſcovered by the moſt exquiſite Art and Cunning, till the bleſſed Reſtauration of His Majeſty to His glorious Throne, ſo filled their Hearts with Joy, that it broke open the Door of their Lips, and let their Tongue loſe to tell this Miracle to the amazed World, would (were not the Perſons yet alive, and the Story freſh in Memory) ratify it into a Romance.

THE Reproaches and Scandals, by which ſome envious Perſons have ſought to diminiſh and vilify the faithful Services, which the Colonel, out of the Integrity of his Soul, performed unto His Majeſty, ſhall not here be mentioned ; becauſe by taking up Dirt to beſpatter him, they defile their own Hands, and the Gun they level at

his

his Reputation, recoils to the wounding of their own.

THESE Things thus premised, by Way of Introduction, open the Gate, through which you may enter, and in the ensuing Pages (as in several Tables) take a full View of the Particulars.

THE Disguise His Majesty put on, secured him from the Cruelty of His Enemies, but could not altogether hide Him from the prying Eyes of his dutiful Subjects. For in the Time of His Stay at *Leigh*, one *John Pope*, (then Butler to Sir *George Norton*, but formerly a Soldier for the King in the West) through all those Clouds espied the most illustrious Person of the King. With him His Majesty (after He saw Himself discovered) was pleased familiarly to discourse; and speaking of the great Sufferings of very many of His Friends in the Western Parts (most whereof were well known to *Pope)* His Majesty enquired if he knew Colonel *Francis Wyndham*, who, (in the Time of the late Wars) was Governour of *Dunster*-Castle? Very well, Sir, answered *Pope.* The King then demanding what was become of him? *Pope* replies, that the Colonel had married Mrs.

Ann.

Ann Gerrard, one of the Daughters and Heiresses of *Thomas Gerrard*, Esq; late of *Trent* in *Somersetshire*, and that he had newly brought thither his Mother, (the Lady *Wyndham*) his Wife and Family; and that he believed the Colonel intended there to reside and live. His Majesty having received this Intelligence concerning the Colonel, together with an exact Information of the Situation of *Trent*, sought an Opportunity to speak with Mrs. *Lane*, (from whom the better to conceal Himself, He then kept at a distance) and by means of Mr. *Lassels*, (who accompanied the King in this Journey) obtaining his Desire, His Majesty, with much Contentment imparted to Mrs. *Lane* what *Pope* had informed Him concerning Colonel *Wyndham*, and his Habitation; telling her withal, that if she could bring him thither, He should not doubt of His Safety.

In this very Point of Time comes the Lord *Henry Wilmot*, afterwards Earl of *Rochester*, from *Dirham* in *Gloucestershire*, the Seat of *John Winter*, Esq; a Person of known Loyalty and Integrity, to *Leigh*. My Lord had attended His Majesty in His Passage Westward, and on *Friday* Morning, *September* the 13th, met accidentally Captain

tain *Thomas Abington,* of *Dowdſwell,* in
the County of *Glouceſter,* at *Pinbury* Park ;
and being known by the Captain, who had
ſerved under him in the late Wars, was that
Night by him conducted to Mr. *Winter's,*
from whom his Lordſhip (as he hath often
ſince acknowledged) received great Ci-
vilities. Mrs. *Lane* preſently reveals to the
Lord *Wilmot* the King's Reſolution to remove to *Trent* ; whereupon my Lord demanded of *Henry Rogers,* Mr. *Winter's*
Servant, and his Lordſhip's Guide from
Dirham to *Leigh.* Whether he knew *Trent ?*
He anſwered, that Colonel *Wyndham* and
his Maſter had married two Siſters, and
that he had often waited on his Maſter
thither. Theſe Things ſo happily concur-
ring, His Majeſty commanded the Lord
Wilmot to haſte to *Trent,* and to aſcertain
the Colonel of his ſpeedy Approach.

His Lordſhip took Leave, and continu-
ing *Rogers* for his Guide, with one *Robert
Swan,* arrived at *Trent* the ſixteenth of
September. Rogers was ſent in forthwith
to the Colonel, to acquaint him, that a
Gentleman, a Friend of his, deſired the
Favour of him, that he would pleaſe to
ſtep forth and ſpeak with him. The Colo-
nel enquiring of *Rogers* whether he knew
M 3　　　　　the

the Gentleman or his Business? answered, No, he understood nothing at all, but only that he was called by the Name of Mr. *Morton*. Then without farther Discourse, the Colonel came forth, and found the Gentleman walking near the Stable; whom, as soon as he approached, although it was somewhat dark, he saluted by the Title of, My Lord *Wilmot* His Lordship seemed to wonder that he should be known; but it was nothing strange, considering the Colonel's former Acquaintance with him, being one of the first that engaged under his Command in His late Majesty's Service. Besides, his Lordship was not in the least altered, except a Hawk on his Fist, and a Lure by his Side might pass for a Disguise. This Confidence of his-Lordship really begat Admiration in the Colonel, calling to mind the great Danger he was in, and whose Harbinger he was; for he advertised the Colonel, that the King Himself was on His Way to *Trent*, intending that very Night to lodge at *Castle-Cary*, (a Town six Miles thence) hoping, by God's Assistance to be with him about Ten of the Clock next Morning.

At this joyful News the Colonel was transported, (there having run a Report,
that

that His-Majesty was slain in the Fight at *Worcester*) and giving God Thanks for his wonderful Mercy, he assured his Lordship, *That for His Majesty's Preservation he would value neither his Life, Family nor Fortune, and would never injure His Majesty's Confidence of him; not doubting, but that God, who had led his Majesty through the midst of such inexpressible Dangers, would deliver Him from all those barbarous Threats, and bloody Intentions of. His Enemies.* With these and such like Expressions, the Colonel brought the Lord *Wilmot* into his Parlour, where he received an exact Account of His Majesty's Condition and present Affairs.

NEXT Morning the Colonel found it necessary to acquaint the Lady *Wyndham*, his Mother, and also his own Lady, with the Particulars the Lord *Wilmot* had over Night imparted to him, concerning the King. The Relation he gave them, did not (through the Weakness of their Sex) bring upon them any womanish Passion, but surprized with Joy, they most cheerfully resolve, without the least Shew of Fear, to hazard all, for the Safety of the King. And so (begging God's Blessing upon their sincere Endeavours) they contrive how His

Majesty

Majesty might be brought into the House, without any Suspicion to their Family, consisting of above 20 Persons. Among them, therefore Mrs. *Julian Comingsly* (the Lady *Wyndham*'s Niece) *Elianor Withers*, *Joan Halfenoth*, and *Henry Peters*, (whose Loyalty to the King, and Fidelity to themselves, they had sufficiently experienced) are made privy to their Design. Next they consider what Chambers are fittest for His Majesty's Reception. Four are made choice of; amongst which the Lady *Wyndham*'s was counted most convenient for the Daytime, where the Servants might wait with more Freedom upon His Majesty. Then a safe Place is provided to retreat unto, in case of Search, or imminent Danger. And lastly, Employments are designed to remove all others out of the Way at the Instant of His Majesty's Arrival. All which, after a while, answered their Desires, even beyond their Expectation.

BETWEEN nine and ten the next Morning, the Colonel and his Lady walking towards the Fields adjoining to the House, espied the King riding before Mrs. *Lane*, and Mr. *Laffels* in their Company. Affoon as His Majesty came near the Colonel, He called to him, *Frank, Frank, how dost thou do?*

do? By which gracious Pleasance the Colonel perceiv'd, that though his Majesty's Habit and Countenance were much changed, yet his heroic Spirit was the same, and His Mind immutable. The Colonel (to avoid the jealous Eyes of some Neighbours) instantly conveyed the King and Mrs. *Lane* into the Lady *Wyndham's* Chamber, where the Passions of Joy and Sorrow did a while combat in them, who beheld His sacred Person. For what loyal Eye could look upon so glorious a Prince thus eclipsed, and not pay unto Him the Homage of Tears? But the Consideration of His Majesty's Safety, the gracious Words of His own Mouth confuting the sad Reports of his untimely Death, together with the Hope of his future Preservation, soon dried them up. In a short Time the Colonel brought the Lord *Wilmot* to the King, and then the Ladies withdrew into the Parlour, having first agreed to call Mrs. *Lane* Cousin, and to entertain her with the same Familiarity as if she had been their nearest Relation. That Day she stayed at *Trent*, and the next Morning early Mr. *Lassels* and she departed.

HIS Majesty, after He had refreshed Himself, commanded the Colonel in the

Presence of the Lord *Wilmot*, to propose, what Way he thought most probable for His Escape into *France*; for thither He desired with all Speed to be transported. The Colonel (the King giving him this Opportunity) entertained and encouraged His Majesty with this remarkable Passage of Sir *Thomas Wyndham* (his Father) *Who, not long before his Death, (in the Year 1636) called unto him his five Sons (having not seen them together in some Years before) and discoursed unto us (said he) of the loving Peace and Prosperity this Kingdom hath enjoyed under its three last glorious Monarchs: Of the many Miseries and Calamities which lay sore upon our Ancestors, by the several Invasions and Conquests of foreign Nations, and likewise by intestine Insurrections and Rebellions. And notwithstanding the strange Mutations and Changes in England, he shewed how it pleased God, in Love to our Nation, to preserve an undoubted Succession of Kings, to sit on the Royal Throne. He mentioned the healing Conjunction of the two Houses of* York *and* Lancaster, *and the blessed Union of the two Crowns of* England *and* Scotland, *stopping up those Fountains of Blood, which, by national Feuds and Quarrels, kept open, had like to have drowned the whole Island.*

Island. He said, he feared the beautiful Garment of Peace would shortly be torn in pieces through the Neglect of Magistrates, the General Corruption of Manners, and the Prevalence of a puritanical Faction, which, (if not prevented) would undermine the very Pillars of Government. My Sons! we have hitherto seen serene and quiet Times; but now prepare your selves for cloudy and troublesome. I command you to honour and obey our Gracious Sovereign, and in all Times to adhere to the Crown; and though the Crown should hang upon a Bush, I charge you forsake it not. These Words being spoken with much Earnestness, both in Gesture and Manner extraordinary, he rose from his Chair, and left us in a deep Consultation what the Meaning should be of The Crown hanging upon a Bush. These Words, Sir, (said the Colonel) made so firm an Impression on all our Breasts, that the many Afflictions of these sad Times cannot raze out their undelible Characters. Certainly, these are the Days which my Father pointed out in that Expression; and I doubt not, God hath brought me through so many Dangers, that I might shew my self both a dutiful Son, and a loyal Subject, in faithfully endeavour-

ing

ing to serve your sacred Majesty, in this your greatest Distress.

AFTER this Rehearsal, the Colonel (in Obedience to His Majesty's Command) told the King, that Sir *John Strangways* (who had given many Testimonies of his Loyalty, having two Sons, both of them Colonels for his Royal Father) lived but four Miles from *Trent*, that he was a Person of great Fortune and Interest in *Dorsetshire*, and therefore he supposed that either Sir *John* or Sons might be serviceable to His Majesty's Occasions. The King in Prosecution of this Proposal commanded the Colonel to wait on them; and accordingly the next Morning he went over to *Melbury*, the Place where Sir *John* dwelt. No sooner was he come thither, but he met with Colonel *Giles Strangways*, and after usual Salutations, they walked into the Park adjoining to the House, where Colonel *Wyndam* imparted the Reason and End of his present Visit. Colonel *Strangways*'s Answer was, that he was infinitely grieved because he was not able to serve His Majesty in procuring a Vessel according to Expectation; that he knew not any one Master of a Ship, or so much as one Mariner that he could trust: All that were

formerly

formerly of his Acquaintance in *Weymouth*, being for their Loyalty banished, and gone beyond the Sea; and in *Pool* and *Lime* he was a meer Stranger, having not one Confident in either. A hundred Pounds in Gold he delivered to Colonel *Wyndham*, to present to the King; which at his Return, by Command was deposited in the Hands of the Lord *Wilmot*, for His Majesty's Use.

About this Time the Forces under *Cromwell* were retreated from *Worcester* into the several Quarters of the Country; some of which coming to *Trent*, proclaimed the Overthrow of the King's Army, and the Death of the King, giving out, that he was certainly killed; and one of them affirmed that he saw him dead, and that he was buried among the rest of the slain, no Injury being offered to his Body, because he was a valiant Soldier, and a gallant Man. This welcome News so tickled the Sectaries, that they could not hold from expressing their Joy by making Bonfires, firing of Guns, Drinking and other Jollities; and for a Close of all, to the Church they must, and there ring the King's Knell. These rude Extravagancies moved not his Majesty at all, but only (as if he were more trou-

N

bled

bled for their Madneſs, than his own Misfortune) to this moſt Chriſtian and compaſſionate Expreſſion, *Alas, poor People!*

Now, though the King valued not the Menaces of his proud Enemies, being confident they could do him no Hurt; yet he neglected not to try the Faithfulneſs of his Friends to convoy him out of their Reach. Thus the former Deſign proving unſuccesful, and all Hope of Transfretation that Way being laid aſide, the Colonel acquainted his Majeſty, that one Captain *William Elleſden* of *Lime,* (formerly well known unto him) with his Brother *John Elleſden,* (by Means of Colonel *Bullen Reymes* of *Wadden,* in *Dorſetſhire*) had conveyed over into *France* Sir *John Berkley* (afterward Lord *Berkley*) in a Time of Danger. To this Captain therefore his Majeſty ſends the Colonel, who lodging at his Houſe in *Lime,* took an Opportunity to tell him, that the Lord *Wilmot* had made his Eſcape from *Worceſter*; that he lay privately near to him; and that his Lordſhip had earneſtly follicited him to uſe his utmoſt Endeavours to ſecure him from the Hands of the Purſuers. To this Purpoſe he was come to Town, and aſſured the Captain, if he would join in this Affair, his Courteſy

ſhould

should never be forgotten. The Captain very cordially embraced the Motion, and went with the Colonel to *Charmouth*, (a little Place near *Lime*) where at an Inn, he brought to him a Tenant of his, one *Stephen Limbry*, assuring the Colonel, that he was a right honest Man, and a perfect Royalist. With this *Limbry* Colonel *Wyndham* treated under the Name of Captain *Norris*, and agreed with him to transport himself and three or four Friends into *France*. The Conditions of their Agreement were; that before the two and twentieth Day of that Instant *September*, *Limbry* should bring his Vessel into *Charmouth*-Road, and on the said two and twentieth, in the Night, should receive the Colonel and his Company into the Long-Boat from the Beach near *Charmouth*, from thence carry them to his Ship, and so land them safe in *France* This the Colonel conjured *Limbry* to perform with all Secresy, because all the Passegers were of the Royal Party, and intended to be shipped without Leave, to avoid such Oaths and Engagements, which otherwise would be forced upon them; and therefore Privacy in this Transaction would free him from Danger, and themselves from Trouble, the

N 2   true

true Cauſe why they ſo earneſtly thirſted (for ſome Time) to leave their native Country, *Limbry*'s Salary was ſixty Pounds, which the Captain engaged to pay at his Return from *France*, upon Sight of a Certificate under the Paſſengers Hands of their landing there. To the Performance of theſe Covenants, *Limbry*, with many Vows and Proteſtations obliging himſelf, the Colonel with much Satisfaction and Speed, came back to his Majeſty and the Lord *Wilmot* to *Trent*, who, at the Narration of theſe Paſſages expreſſed no ſmall Contentment.

THE Buſineſs being thus far ſucceſsfully laid, the King conſults how it might be prudentially managed, that ſo there might be no Miſcarriage in the Proſecution. Neceſſary it was that his Majeſty and all his Attendants (contrary to the Uſe of Travellers) ſhould ſit up all the Night in the Inn at *Charmouth* ; that they ought to have the Command of the Houſe, to go in and out at Pleaſure, the Tide not ſerving till twelve at Night. To remove therefore all Suſpicion and Inconveniencies, this Expedient was found out.

HENRY *Peters* (Colonel *Wyndham*'s Servant) was ſent to *Charmouth* Inn, who inviting the Hoſteſs to drink a Glaſs of Wine,

Wine, told her, that he served a very gallant Master, who had long, most affectionately loved a Lady in *Devon*, and had the Happiness to be well beloved by her; and though her Equal in Birth and Fortune, yet so unequal was his Fate, that by no Means could he obtain her Friends Consent: And therefore it was agreed between them, that he should carry her thence, and marry her among his own Allies. And for this Purpose his Master had sent him to desire her to keep the best Chambers for him, intending to be at her House upon the two and twentieth Day of that Month in the Evening, where he resolved not to lodge, but only to refresh himself and Friends, and so travel on either that Night, or very early next Morning. With this Love-Story (thus contrived and acted) together with a Present delivered by *Peters* from his Master, the Hostess was so well pleased, that she promised him, her House and Servants should be at his Master's Command. All which she very justly performed.

WHEN the Day appointed for Majesty's Journey to *Charmouth* was come, he was pleased to ride before Mrs. *Julian Coningsby*, (the Lady *Wyndham*'s Niece) as formerly before Mrs. *Lane*. The Colonel was his Majesty's Guide, whilst the Lord *Wilmot* with *Peters* kept at a convenient Distance, that they might not seem to be all of one Company.

In this Manner travelling, they were timely met by Captain *Ellesden*, and by him conducted to a private House of his Brother's among the Hills near *Charmouth*. There his Majesty was pleased to discover himself to the Captain, and to give him a Piece of foreign Gold, in which in his solitary Hours he made a Hole to put a Ribbon in. Many like Pieces his Majesty vouchsafed the Colonel and his Lady, to be kept as Records of his Majesty's Favour, and of their own Fidelity to his most sacred Person in the Day of his greatest Trial. All which they have most thankfully treasured up as the chiefest Jewels of their Family.

This Royal Company from thence came to the Inn at *Charmouth*, a little after Night, where Captain *Ellesden* solemnly engaging to see the Master of the Ship ready, (the Wind blowing then fair for *France*) took Leave of his Majesty. About an Hour after came *Limbry* to the Inn, and assured the Colonel all Things were prepared, and that about Midnight his Long-Boat should wait at the Place appointed. The set Hour drawing

nigh

nigh, the Colonel with *Peters*, went to the Sea-side (leaving his Majesty and the Lord *Wilmot* in a Posture to come upon Call) where they remained all Night expecting; but seeing no Long-Boat, neither hearing any Message from the Master of the Ship, at the Break of Day the Colonel returns to the Inn, and beseeches the King and the Lord *Wilmot* to haste from thence. His Majesty was intreated; but the Lord *Wilmot* was desirous to stay behind a little, promising to follow the King to *Bridport*, where his Majesty intended to make a Halt for him.

WHEN the King was gone, the Lord *Wilmot* sent *Peters* into *Lime*, to demand of Captain *Ellesden*, the Reason why *Limbry* broke his Promise, and forfeited his Word? He seemed much surprized with this Message, and said, he knew no Reason, except it being a fair Day, the Seamen were drunk in taking their Farewel; and withal advised his Lordship to be gone, because his Stay there could not be safe. But since that, *Limbry* himself hath given this Account under his own Hand :——

THAT according to an Agreement made at *Charmouth*, *September* the 19th, 1651, betwixt himself and one Captain *Norris*,

(since

(fince known to be Colonel *Francis Wynd-ham*) he put forth the Ship beyond the *Cobs-mouth* into *Charmouth-Road*, where his Servants on the 22d of the fame Month were all ready in her, waiting his coming; that he going to his Houfe about ten that Night, for Linnen to carry with him, was unexpectedly locked into a Chamber by his Wife, to whom he had a little before revealed his intended Voyage with fome Paffengers into *France*, for whofe Tranfportation, at his Return, he was to receive a confiderable Sum of Money from Captain *Elle,den*.

THIS Woman, it feems, was frighted into a pannick Fear by that dreadful *Proclamation* (of the 10th of *September*) fet out by the *Men of Weftminfter*, and publifhed that Day at *Lime*. In this a heavy Penalty was thundered out againft all that fhould conceal the King, or any of his Party, who were at *Worcefter* Fight; and a Reward of a Thoufand Pounds promifed to any that fhould betray him. She, apprehending the Perfons her Husband engaged to carry over to be Royalifts, refolved to fecure him from Danger, by making him a Prifoner in his own Chamber. All the Perfuafions he ufed for his Liberty ty were in vain ; for the more he intreated, the more her violent Paffion increafed, breaking forth into fuch Clamours and Lamentations, that he feared if he fhould any longer contend, both himfelf and the Gentlemen he promifed to tranfport, would be caft away in this Storm, without ever going to Sea.

THUS a Defign in a Bufinefs of the higheft Nature, and carried on with Induftry and Prudence, even to the very laft, ftill promifing full Hope of a happy Production, by one Man's fingle Whifper (the Bane of Action) proved abortive. For, no Doubt, had *Limbry* kept his Council, he had gained the Honour of conveying over his Majefty ; of whofe noble Courage and Virtue, God was pleafed to make yet farther Trial, as the Sequel will inform.

THE King paffing on upon *London*-Road from *Charmouth*, met many Travellers, among whom was one of his Father's Servants, well known both to his Majefty and the Colonel ; who were very well pleafed that he was not guilty of fo much Civility, as to give either of them the Compliment of a Salutation. As they drew near to *Bridport*, the Colonel riding a little before, and

and entering the Town, perceived it full of
Soldiers ; whereupon stopping his Horse
till the King came up, he intreated his Majesty to keep on, and by no Means to put
himself into the Mouth of them, who ga-
ped greedily after his Destruction. Never-
theless, the King having engaged to the
Lord *Wilmot*, to expect him there, (without the least Apprehension of Danger)
rode into the *George*, and alighting in the
Court, was forced to stay there, and in the
Stable, near half an Hour, before the Colonel could procure a Chamber. All this
While his bloody Enemies were his only
Companions, with whom he discoursed freely without Fear, and learned from them
their intended Voyage for *Jersey* and *Guern-
sey*, and their Design upon those Islands.
Here may you see the Pursuers overtaken,
and the bitterest of Enemies friendly dis-
coursing with him, whose utter Ruin they
accounted would compleat their Happiness.
He that sate in Heaven, certainly laughed
them to Scorn, and by the Interposition of
his mighty Arm eclipsed their Glory, and
by his admirable Wisdom reproved and
confuted their Malice against the King, and
their Blasphemies against Heaven.

No

No sooner had the King withdrawn himself from this dangerous Company, into a Chamber, (with much Difficulty obtained) acquainted his Majesty, that the Lord *Wilmot* humbly petitioned him to make Haste out of that Place, and to overtake him flowly paffing on the Road, and waiting his Majesty's coming. Prefently upon the Difmiffion of *Peters,* the King having taken fome fmall Repaft, not far from the Town joined in Company again with the Lord *Wilmot,* and difcourfing of the feveral Adventures of that hopeful, and (as it fell out) moft perilious Journey, concluded that *London*-Road was very unfafe, and therefore refolved to follow the next Turning which might probably lead towards *Yeavill,* or *Sherborn,* neither of which is computed to be above two Miles diftant from *Trent.* Providence (the beft of Guides) directed thefe Strangers (for fo they were all in thofe Parts) to a Way, which after many Hours Travel brought them into a Village, in which was a fmall Inn for Entertainment. Thus entered thefe masked Travellers, to enquire where they were. And to this Purpofe calling for fome Beer, the Hoft of the Houfe (one *Rice Jones*) came forth, and informed

ed them, that the Place was called *Broad-windfor*. The Colonel knew the Innkeeper and his Wife to be very honeft, loyal Perfons, and that for their Fidelity to the King and his Party, they had (according to their Condition) undergone their Share of Troubles. The King underftanding the Affection of the People, refolves to lodge in the Houfe that Night, it being already fomewhat dark, and his Majefty, and Company, fufficiently wearied with their former Night's Watching, and that Day's Travel. The Colonel (while the Horfes were put up) defired Mr. *Jones* to fhew him the moft private Rooms; the Reafon he gave was, becaufe his Brother-in-Law, Colonel *Reymes* (whom the Lord *Wilmot* perfonated) had been a long Time imprifoned as well as himfelf; that they had lately obtained their Paroles, and to be feen together fo far from their Homes might create new Jealoufies, and fo confequently crufh them with new Troubles. The good Hoft upon this, brought them up into the higheft Chambers, where Privatenefs recompenfed the Meannefs of the Accommodation, and the Pleafantnefs of the Hoft (a merry Fellow) allayed and mitigated the Wearinefs of the Guefts. Now the Face
of

of Things began to smile, which all the Day
and Night preceding, looked so louring and
ill-favoured : But this short Calm was on a
sudden interrupted by a violent Storm.
For in comes the Constable with almost forty
Soldiers to be billeted that very Night in
the Inn ; all the lower Receptacles were
thronged up with this unexpected Company ; so that the King was in a Manner be-
sieged, there being no Passage, from above,
but through those suspected Guards.　Thus
every Place brought forth its Troubles, and
every Period of Time disclosed fresh Dangers ! Shortly after the Soldiers had taken
up their Quarters, a Woman in their Company fell into Labour in the Kitchen.　The
Pangs she endured, made the Inhabitants
of that Place very ill at Ease, fearing left
the whole Parish should become the reputed
Father, and be enforced to keep the Child.
To avoid this Charge, the chiefest of the
Parish post to the Inn, between whom, and
the Soldiers, arose a very hot Conflict, concerning Provision to be made for the Mother and the Infant.　This Dispute continued till such Time as (according to Orders) they were to march to the Sea-Side.
This quarrelsome Gossipping was a most
seasonable Diversion, exercising the Minds
O　　　　　　of

of thofe troublefome Fellows, who other-wife were likely to have proved too too inquifitive after the Guefts in the Houfe; the fad Confequences of which, every loyal Heart trembles to think on.

Surely we cannot, except we wilfully fhut our own Eyes, but clearly fee, and with all Reverence and Thankfulnefs adore the divine Goodnefs for his Majefty's fignal Deliverances in this Voyage: Efpecially if, looking back upon *Charmouth*, we con-fider the Dangers that threaten'd him, oc-cafioned by the Lord *Wilmot*'s fhort Stay there, after the King's Departure; for one *Hamnet*, a Smith, being call'd to fhoe his Lordfhip's Horfe, faid, he well knew by the Fafhion of the Shoes, that they were never fet in the Weft, but in the North. The Hoftler, a Bird of the fame Feather, hearing this, began to tell, what Company had been there; how they fat up, and kept their Horfes faddled all the Night: And from hence they conclude, that either the King, or fome great Perfons had cer-tainly been at the Inn. The Hoftler, whofe Heart was foured againft the King, runs prefently to one *Weftly*, of the fame Leaven, then Minifter of *Charmouth*, to inform him of thefe Paffages, and, to afk Counfel what

was

was to done. This *Weſtley*, was at his Morning Exerciſe, and being ſomething long-winded, *and by the Way it may be obſerved, that long Prayers proceeding from a traiterous Heart, once did good, but by Accident only,* the Hoſtler unwilling to loſe his Reward, at the Gentleman's taking Horſe, returns without doing his Errand. As ſoon as my Lord was mounted and gone, *Hamnet* tells *Weſtley* of the Diſcourſe between him and the Hoſtler. Away comes *Weſtley* upon full Speed to the Inn, and almoſt out of Breath, asks the Woman of the Houſe, what Gueſts ſhe had entertained that Night? She ſaid, they were all Strangers to her, ſhe knew them not. I tell you then, ſaid he, one of them was the King. Then haſtily turning away from her, he and *Hamnet* ran to Mr. *Butler* of *Commer*, then Juſtice of Peace, to have diſpatched abroad his Warrants to raiſe the Country for the apprehending of the King, and thoſe Perſons, the laſt Night, with him at *Charmouth*: But he ſpends his Mouth in vain, a deaf Ear is turned upon him, no Warrant would be iſſued forth. This Check given to his Zeal ſo vexed him, that it had like to have cauſed a Suffocation, had not Captain *Maſſey*, as errant a Hotſpur as himſelf, given it

O 2   Vent

Vent by raising a Party, and pursuing the King upon *London*-Road. But God preserved his Majesty by diverting him to *Broadwindsor*, whilst *Massey* and his hot-mettled Company out-ran their prey as far as *Dorchester*. And indeed, the Report of the King's being at *Charmouth*, was grown so common, that the Soldiers, lying in those Parts, searched the Houses of several Gentlemen who were accounted Royalists, thinking to surprize him. Amongst which, *Pilisdon*, the House of Sir *Hugh Wyndham*, Uncle to Colonel *Francis Wyndham*, was twice rifled. They took the old Baronet, his Lady, Daughters and whole Family, and set a Guard upon them in the Hall, whilst, they examine every Corner, not sparing either trunk or Box. Then taking a particular View of their Prisoners, they seize a lovely young Lady, saying, she was the King disguised in Woman's Apparel. At length being convinced of their gross and rude Mistake, they desisted from offering any further Violence to that Family. And here it is much to be observed, that the same Day the King went from *Charmouth*, Captain *Elesden* came to *Pilisdon*, and enquired of Sir *Hugh* and his Lady, for the King

King and Colonel, confidently affirming, that they muft needs be there.

His Majefty having with an Evennefs of Spirit, gotten through this rough Paffage, fafely anchor'd at *Broadwindfor*, where at length enjoying fome Reft, he commands the Colonel to give his Opinion what Courfe was to be taken, as the Face of Affairs then looked. The Colonel (feeing Forces drawn every where upon that Shore) thought it very hazardous to attempt any Thing mo e in *Dorfetfhire*; and therefore humbly befought His Majefty, that he would be pleaf ed to retreat to *Trent*: He hoped His Majefty was already fatisfied in the Fidelity of his Servants; and that he doubted not, His Majefty might lie fecurely in that Creek, 'till it was fair Weather, and a good Seafon to put forth to Sea. He humbly advifed, that *Peters* might conduct the Lord *Wilmot* to Mr. *Hutt*'s Houfe at the *King's-Arms* in *Sarum*, where he and many of his Friends had been fheltered in the Time of Troubles. That *Peters* (being at *Sarum*) fhould by a private Token bring his Lordfhip to Mr. *John Coventry*, (his Kinfman) a Perfon noble, wife, and loyal, with whom he had kept Intelligence in Order to the King's Service, ever fince His

Majefty

Majesty had set Foot in *Scotland* ; that he
was assured Mr. *Coventry* would think himself highly honoured to correspond in this
matchless Employment, *The King's Preservation*. He desired the Lord *Wilmot* to be
confident of lying concealed ; and likewise
to treat with Mr. *Coventry*, and by *Peters*
to return His Majesty an Account how he
found that Gentleman affected towards this
Service.

THIS Counsel being well relished and
approved, it was resolved, that between
Sarum and *Trent*, (lying thirty Miles distant, and better) an Intercourse should be
kept by trusty Messengers, and a secret
Way of writing, to avoid Danger in case of
Interception. All Things being thus concluded, the King left his jovial Host at
Broadwinsor, and returned with the Colo-
nel and Mrs. *Coningsby* to *Trent*. The
Lord *Wilmot* with *Peters* went that Night
to *Sherborn*, and the next Morning was
waited on by *Swan*, who attended his
Lordship to the Colonel's, and that Day
got into *Sarum*, where he soon saluted Mr.
Coventry, in all Things fully answering his
Lordship's Expectation : And the 25th of
September, *Peters* was sent back with this
joyful Message from the Lord *Wilmot* to his
Majesty

Majesty; that he doubted not, by Mr.
Coventry's Assistance, and those recommended by him, to be able in some short Time
to effect his Desires.

Whilst his sacred Majesty enjoys his
Peace at *Trent*, and the Lord *Wilmot*, with
those other Worthies, is busied at *Sarum*,
to produce its Continuation: It cannot be
impertinent to mention a Circumstance or
two, which inserted in the midst of the
Web and Texture of this Story, would have
looked unhandsome, but added as a Fringe,
may prove ornamental.

Upon the *Sunday* Morning after the King
came to *Trent*, a Taylor of the Parish informed the Colonel, that the Zealots, which
swarmed in that Place, discoursed over
Night, that Persons of Quality were hid
in his House, and that they intended to
search and seize them; and therefore he desired the Colonel, if any such there were,
to convey them thence, to avoid Surprisal.
The Colonel, rewarding the good Man for
his Care and Kindness towards himself and
Family, told him, that his Kinsman, meaning the Lord *Wilmot*, was not private, but
public in his House, for so his Lordship
pleased to be, and that he believed he would
shew himself in the Church, at the Time of
Prayers.

Prayers. When the honest Fellow was gone, the Colonel acquaints the King what passed between himself and the Taylor, and withal, besought his Majesty to persuade the Lord *Wilmot* to accompany him to Church, thinking by this Means, not only to lessen the Jealousy, but also to gain the good Opinion of some of the Fanaticks, who would be apt to believe, that the Colonel was rather brought to Church by my Lord, than his Lordship by the Colonel, who seldom came to that Place, since Faction and Rebellion had justled out, and kept Possession against Peace and Religion. He alledged moreover, that he sat in an Ile distinct from the Body of the Congregation, so that the Parishioners could not take a full View of any of his Company. These Reasons, joined with his Majesty's Command, prevailed with his Lordship; and though he thought it a bold Adventure, yet, it not only allayed the Fury, but also took out the very Sting of those Wasps; insomuch, that they, who the last Night talked of nothing but searching, began now to say, that *Cromwell*'s late Success against the King, had made the Colonel a Convert.

ALL

ALL being now quiet about Home, the Colonel's Lady, under a Pretence of a Visit, goes over to *Sherbon*, to hear what News there was abroad of the King. And towards Evening, at her Return, a Troop of Horse clapt privately into the Town. This silent Way of entering their Quarters, in so triumphant a Time, gave a strong alarm to this careful Lady; whose Thoughts were much troubled concerning her Royal Guest. A Stop she made to hearken out what brought them thither, and whither they were bound : But not one Grain of Intelligence could be procured by the most industrious Enquiry. When she came Home, she gave his Majesty an Account of many Stories, which like flying Clouds, were blown about by the Breath of the People, striving to cover her Trouble with the Vail of Chearfulness. But this the King perceiving to be rather forced than free, as at other Times, was earnest to know the Cause of her Discomposure. And to satisfy his Majesty's Importunity, she gave him a full Relation of the Troop at *Sherbon* : At which his Majesty laughed most heartily, as if he had not been in the least concerned. Yet, upon a serious Debate of the Matter, the Colonel

lonel and his Lady fupplicated the King to take a View of his privy Chamber, into which he was perfuaded to enter, but came prefently forth again, much pleafed, that upon the leaft Approach of Danger, he could thither retreat with an Affurance of Security.   All that Night the Colonel kept ftrict Watch in his Houfe, and was the more vigilant, becaufe he underftood from *Sherbon*, that the Troop intended not to Quarter there, but only to refrefh themfelves and march. And accordingly (not fo much as looking towards *Trent*) about two of the Clock the next Morning, they removed towards the Sea-Coaft. This Fear being over, the King refted all the Time of his Stay at *Trent*, without fo much as the Apprehenfion of a Difturbance.

THE Strangenefs of which will be much increafed by the Addition of what a Captain who ferved under *Cromwell*, at *Worcefter*, reported to two Divines of undoubted Veracity, long before the King's bleffed Reftauration: That he was followed and troubled with Dreams for three Nights together, that the King was hid at *Trent*, near *Sherborn*, in a Houfe nigh to which ftood a Grove, or patch of Trees, and that thither he fhould go and find Him. This

This Suggestion thus reiterated, was a powerful Spur to prick him forwards: But the Hand which held the Reins, and kept him back, was irresistible.

Now the Hands of his Majesty's Enemies were not only restrained from doing him Evil, but the Hands of his Friends were strengthened to do him Good. In Order to which, Colonel *Edward Philips* of *Montacute*, in the County of *Somerset*, came from *Sarum*, to his Majesty, *September* the 28th, with this Intelligence, that his Brother Colonel *Robert Philips* was employed to *Southampton* to procure a Vessel, of whose Transaction his Majesty should receive a speedy Account.

In the mean Time, Captain *Thomas Littleton*, a Neighbour of Colonel *Wyndham*, was dispached up into *Hampshire*, where by the Aid of Mr. *Standish*, he dealt with the Master of a Ship, who undertook to cary off the Lord *Wilmot*, and his Company, upon the Condition his Lordship would follow his Direction. But the Hope of Colonel *Philips's* his good Success at *Hampton*, dashed this Enterprise, and the Captain was remanded back to *Trent*, and to make no Progress till farther Orders.

UPON

UPON the firſt of *October*, Mr. *John Selliock*, Chaplain to Mr. *Coventry*, brought a Letter to his Majeſty. In anſwer to which the King wrote back, that he defired all Dilligence might be uſed in providing a Veſſel; and if it ſhould prove difficult at *Hampton*, Trial ſhould be made farther: That they ſhould be afcertained of a Ship before they ſent to remove him, that ſo he might run no more Hazards than what of Neceſſity he muſt meet with in his Paſſage from *Trent* to the Place of his Tranſportation.

OCTOBER the fifth, Colonel *Philips* came from the Lord *Wilmot* and Mr. *Coventry* to his Majeſty with this Aſſurance, that all Things were ready; and that he had informed himſelf with the moſt private Ways, ſo that he might with greater Probability of Safety guide his Majeſty to the Sea-ſide. As ſoon as the King heard this Meſſage, he reſolved upon his Journey. Colonel *Wyndham* earneſtly petitions his Majeſty, that he might wait on him to the Shore: But his Majeſty gave no grant, ſaying, It was no Way neceſſary, and might prove very inconvenient. Upon the renewing this Requeſt, the King demanded the contrary, but ſweetned his Denial with this Promiſe, that if he

were

were put to any Diftrefs, he would again retreat to *Trent*.

ABOUT ten next Morning, *October* the fixth, his Majefty took leave of the old Lady *Wyndham*, the Colonel's Lady, and Family, not omitting the meaneft of them that ferved him : But to the good old Lady he vouchfafed more than ordinary Refpect, who recounted it her higheft Honour, that fhe had three Sons and one Grand-Child flain in the Defence of the Father, and that fhe, herfelf, in her old Age had been in-ftrumental in the Protection of the Son, both Kings of *England*.

THUS his facred Majefty, taking Mrs. *Juliana Coningsby* behind him, attended by Colonel *Robert Philips*, and *Peters*, bad Farewel to *Trent*, the Ark in which God fhut him up, when the Floods of Rebellion had covered the Face of his Dominions. Here he refted nineteen Days, to give his faithful Servants Time to work his Deliverance : And the Almighty crowned their Endeavours with Succefs, that his Majefty might live to appear as Glorious in his Actions, as Couragious in his Sufferings.

F I N I S.

P

By the *Parliament*.

A Proclamation for the Difcovery and Apprehending CHARLES STUART, and other Traytors, his Adherents and Abettors.

WHEREAS, CHARLES STUART, Son to the late Tyrant, with divers of the English and Scottish Nation, have lately, in traitorous and hoftile Manner, with an Army, invaded this Nation, which, by the Bleffing of God upon the Forces of this Common-wealth, have been defeated, and many of the chief Actors therein flain, and taken Prifoners ; but the faid CHARLES STUART is efcaped: For the fpeedy apprehending of fuch a malicious and dangerous Traytor, to the Peace of this Common-wealth, the Parliament doth ftraitly charge and command all Officers, as well Civil as Military, and all other the good People of this Nation, That they make diligent Search and Enquiry for the faid CHARLES STUART, and his Abettors, and Adherents in this Invafion ; and ufe their beft Endeavours for the Difcovery and Arrefting the Bodies of them, and every of them ; and being apprehended, to bring and caufe to be brought forthwith and with-

out

out Delay, in safe Custody, before the Parliament, or Council of State, to be proceeded with, and ordered, as Justice shall require: And if any Person shall knowingly conceal the said CHARLES STUART, or any his Abettors or Adherents, or shall not reveal the Places of their Abode, or Being, if it be in their Power so to do, The Parliament doth declare, that they will hold them as Partakers and Abettors of their traiterous and wicked Practices and Designs: And the Parliament doth further publish and declare, That whosoever shall apprehend the Person of the said CHARLES STUART, and shall bring, or cause him to be brought to the Parliament, or Council of State, shall have given or bestowed on him, or them, as a Reward for such Service, the Sum of One Thousand Pounds: And all Officers, Civil and Military, are required to be aiding and assisting unto such Person and Persons therein. Given at Westminster this Tenth Day of September, One Thousand Six Hundred Fifty One.

Ordered by the Parliament, That this Proclamation be forthwith printed and published.

Hen. Scobel, Cler. Parl.

London, Printed by John Field, Printer to the Parliament of England. 1651.

A

A

SUPPLEMENT

TO

BOSCOBEL.

THE foregoing Relation having brought his Majesty safe into *France*, it may not now be improper to give a short Recapitulation of the most memorable Transactions in *England*, till his happy Restoration. But we may first observe, that not one Dissenter, or Fanatick, was any Way concerned in this wonderful Preservation of his Majesty ; the first we have seen were *Roman* Catholicks, *viz.* Colonel *Giffard*, Colonel *Careless*, the four *Penderels*, and their Brother-in-law *Yates*, the Wife of

this

this laft ; Mr. *Whitgrave* and his Mother ;
Mr. *Wolfe*, and Mr. *Hudleſton* the Prieſt, beſides others, whoſe Names have not been
preſerv'd.   That theſe were all *Roman* Catholicks, is undeniable ; and their Families
continue ſuch to this Day. Colonel *Careleſs*
for his Fidelity, had his Name changed into *Carlos*, and an honourable Addition made
to his Coat of Arms, as it has been before
related : The *Penderels* and *Yates* had each
an hundred Pounds a Year ſettled on them
and their Heirs for ever : And Mr. *Hudleſton*, the Prieſt, had alſo an hundred Pounds
per Annum allow'd him for his Life, and
was by Name excepted in all Acts of Parliament made againſt Prieſts and *Roman* Catholicks, and particular Protection, as to
the Point of Religion, was granted to the
others concern'd in that Loyal Service to
his Majeſty, when the reſt of the *Roman*
Catholicks ſuffer'd for Conſcience Sake.
From the Time of the King's being put into the Hands of Colonel *Lane*, all the reſt
were ſincere Profeſſors of the Doctrine of
the Church of *England*, as preſerv'd in its
Purity, without the Innovations ſome have
ſince labour'd to introduce, by blending its
Principles with thoſe of all Sectaries, hoping thereby to make it a mere *Babel*, that
its

its true Flock may not be diftinguifhed from other fpurious Herds, and that the Sheep and the Goats may be brought into the fame Fold; to which End, many Wolves in Sheeps Cloathing have intruded themfelves, and thofe Thieves, who could not get in at the Door, have broke in at the Windows. But it is eafy to diftinguifh between Hypocrify and true Religion; and tho' a counterfeit Zeal may for fome Time ferve to bring about wicked Defigns, yet Juftice will at laft prevail, as may appear by this Relation; we will therefore proceed to what enfued after what has been above-mentioned.

OLIVER Cromwell, the famous Rebel-General, having, after the Battle of *Worcefter*, reduc'd *Scotland* by Force of Arms, an Union between the two Nations was prefently projected; and tho' the like had been in vain attempted in the Reign of King JAMES the Firft, yet it was now brought about; and, by Confent of the Rebels of both Nations, it was agreed, that *England* and *Scotland* fhould be incorporated into one Common-wealth; as in Effect they were. Next *Cromwell*, who had fecur'd the Army, compofed of canting Hypocrites, the Officers being moft Enthufiaftick

ftick Preachers, and be their chief *Mufti*, turned out that infamous Affembly, which had fo long affumed the Name of a Parliament, and picking out an hundred and forty-four Monfters as vile as the former, from the feveral Counties of *England*, being all outragious Fanaticks, put them into the Place of the others before expelled, where the firft Thing they did, was to ftile themfelves *The Parliament of* England. Then falling upon a thorough Reformation, they declar'd Priefthood to be downright *Popery:* the paying of Tythes *Judaifm*; the Laws of *England*, the Remains of the *Norman* Yoke; Schools and Colleges, Heathen Seminaries; and Nobility and Honours, contrary to Nature and Chriftianity; all which they were for fuppreffing: and actually did abolifh all Courts of Judicature, and appointed all Perfons to be married by Juftices of the Peace.

HAVING thus run the Nation into the utmoft Confufion, they, as had been before concerted, fet up *Cromwell* to tyrannize over the Nation by the Title of *Protector*, with more than regal Power, for they allow'd him a ftanding Army of ten Thoufand Horfe, and fifteen Thoufand Foot. In the Year 1653, that *Ufurper* took the

Govern-

Government upon him, and held it to his Death, which happened on the 3d of *September* 1659. During that Time the Nation fuffered more, as is ufual under all *Ufurpers*, than it had ever done before, or did fince, under the moft pretended Arbitrarinefs of its rightful Monarchs. Yet fuch is the Spirit of Rebellion, that no Examples of paft Calamities are of Force to lay it ; nor can Traytors ever be made fenfible how much eafier they are under the worft of lawful Kings, than under the moft indulgent of Intruders, any longer than the very Moment they groan under the infupportable Burdens laid on them by the Hand of a Tyrant, whom they have unjuftly thruft into the Throne, thro' their own Malice and Folly, and whom Providence often fuffers to fit there long, for the Punifhment of the Villains that raifed him, as may be feen in many Inftances, and particularly this of *Oliver Cromwell*.

UNDER him, Loyalty was Treafon, and Hypocrify paffed for Godlinefs ; his Government was defpotical ; he fpar'd none that were but fufpected to bear him Illwill, and difpofed of their Lives and Eftates at Pleafure ; *England* was by him divided into Provinces, under fo many Major-Generals,

nerals, whofe Power was unlimited, being his own Creatures, and only accountable to him, who was fure to connive at all their Villainies, to fecure them to his Party. The immenfe Sums of Money raifed by him and his Predeceffors in Ufurpation, by the Name of a *Parliament*, far exceed all that the true Sovereigns of *England* had ever receiv'd fince the Conqueft; for it is a moft certain Obfervation, that every fucceffive Rebellion brings greater Oppreffion with it, than any of the former; becaufe *Traytors* and *Ufurpers* continually improve upon one another, not only in the Methods of eftablifhing their ill-gotten Power, but alfo in racking the People, as well to keep them humble, as to heap to themfelves Treafure, to fupport their Authority, and to fecure a Retreat in cafe of Need; becaufe every one of them knowing himfelf to be no better than a Robber, is in perpetual Dread that the rightful Owner will one Time or other recover his own. Let fuch Mifcreants pretend what they will, as to Titles and Claims, in order to blind the Ignorant, they cannot fo much deceive themfelves, but that their own Guilt keeps them upon a perpetual Rack, and is a Worm gnawing their Bowels; though *Satan* has fo great

an

an Influence as never to permit them to repent and do Justice to the injured Sufferers, yet Providence, in its own Time, will bring them to Confusion; for having made Use of them as a Rod to chastise the Sins of the People, they are at last despised, abhorred, and cast into the Fire.

DEATH having put a Period to *Oliver's* Tyranny, his Son *Richard* next stept into the Throne, was solemnly proclaimed and complimented from all Parts of the Nation, with a Multitude of *Addresses*, as has been frequently practised. Many have laboured to persuade the World, that this Wretch had no Inclination to accept of the Government; but these were meer Flights of others like him, who are ever for extolling, or where they dare not, for excusing of all *Usurpers*. Nothing is more certain, than that he was proud of that false Grandeur; that he held it as long as he was able, and that he quitted it not by his good Will, but was ignominiously cast out by the same Instruments who had contributed to exalt his Father and himself; Providence so ordering, that there might be nothing but Confusion and Anarchy, till Justice again took Place.

RICHARD

RICHARD being thus expelled, at the End of a few Months, the next Monster in Power was the *Rump*, made up of forty-two of the virulent Members of the former *Rebel-House of Commons*, whose Names are fit to be preserved as a Monument of Infamy, and were, the Lord *Munster*, Harry *Martin*, *Whitelock*, *Lisle*, *Thomas Chaloner*, Alderman *Atkins*, Alderman *Pennington*, *Thomas Scot*, *Cornelius Holland*, Sir *Henry Vane*, *Prideaux*, Sir *James Harrington*, Lieutenant-General *Ludlow*, *Michael Oldsworth*, Sir *Arthur Haslerig*, *Jones*, Colonel *Purefoy*, Colonel *White*, Harry *Nevil*, *Say*, *Blagrave*, Colonel *Bennet*, *Brewster*, Serjeant *Wild*, *John Goodwin*, *Nicholas Lechmere*, *Augustin Skinner*, *Downes*, *Dove*, *John Lenthal*, *Saloway*, *John Corbet*, *Walton*, *Gilbert Willington*, *Gold*, Colonel *Sydenham*, Colonel *Bingham*, Colonel *Ayre*, *Smith*, Colonel *Ingoldsby*, and Lieutenant-General *Fleetwood*. These being got into the House of Commons, kept the Possession to themselves, excluding fourteen others as good as themselves, who would also have crowded in. They presently voted, that none should sit there who had not sate since the Year 1648; not that they thought the others any honester than themselves,

felves, but becaufe it was more advantageous to themfelves, being fo few in Number, to govern all. Next they appointed a
Council of State, as they called it, to dif-
pofe of all the Places of Profit and Truft,
and of the Treafure of the Nation, whofe
Names are alfo fit to be remembred ; for
by Names, good Obfervations may be
made ; they were, Sir *Arthur Haflerig*, Sir
*Henry Vane, Ludlow, J. Jones, Sydenham,
Scot, Saloway, Fleetwood, Harrington, Wal-
cot, Nevil, Chaloner, Downes, Whitelock,
Morley, Sydney, Thompfon, Dixwell, Reynolds, St. John, Wallop, Bradfhaw, Lambert, Desborcugh, Fairfax, Berry,* Sir *Anthony Afhley Cooper,* afterwards Earl of
Shaftsbury, Sir *Horatio Townfhend,* Sir *Robert Honeywood,* Sir *Archibald Johnfon,* and
Jofiah Berners. Now, there being no fu-
rer Support for Villainy, than Superftition,
thofe Mifcreants appointed a Day of fafting ; and to fhew their Malice to the King
and his Friends, whom they ftill feared,
one of them could not forbear, upon that
Occafion, expreffing himfelf in thefe Words.
*The Lord ftir up the Hearts of his People to
Prayer, and fincere Humiliation, and fill
them with Unanimity and Courage, in this
evil Time, and make the People to fec, that*
                                              whatever

whatever fair Pretences may be made Ufe of by the common *Enemy, to get Power into their Hands, yet fhould they prevail, no Man that has been of a Party againft them beretofore, yea, no Man that has been a mere Neuter, but muft expect that his private Eftate, as well as the publick Liberty, fhall become a Prey to a defperate Crew of ravenous and unreafonable Men; for let but* CHARLES STUART *get in, and then to fatisfy the Rabble of Followers, and the Payment of Foreigners to enflave you, you fhall foon fee them entail'd upon your felves and your Pofterity, to maintain the Pomp and Pride of a luxurious Court, and an abfolute Tyranny.*

OBSERVE here the Language of *Rebels;* fee what abominable Notions are inculcated to render a rightful Monarch odious. But they did not ftop here, for the rifing in *Chefhire,* under Sir *George Booth,* having been fupprefs'd by *Lambert,* thofe hellifh *Saints* proceeded in flandering the Royal Family in a moft outragious Manner; and to crown all Villainies, after having murdered fo many for Loyalty, they invented a Method to damn their Souls, if by ill Ufage they could draw them into the Snare, which was by an *Abjuration-Oath,* to be

Q   rammed

rammed down the Throats of all Perfons, and was in the following Words.

I A. B. do hereby declare, that I renounce the pretended Title *of* Charles Stuart, *and the whole Line of the late King* James, &c.

These People would not allow of Titles, or that Prince any Right to the Crown, and yet they call'd him by his Name, not King or Prince, but Charles Steuart, thereby owning him to be the Son of King Charles the Firft; though they also fometimes call'd him the *Pretender*. It is true, fome private Villains had the Impudence to revile the Queen his Mother, a Princefs of untainted Virtue; but that ufurping Government never proceeded to attack her Reputation; they would have murdered her Son, as they had before her Husband, but did not deny him to be lawfully begotten.

To proceed, the *Rump*, which had begun to lord it, and fet on Foot the abovementioned horrid *Abjuration-Oath*, falling out with the Army, were themfelves, in *October*, turned out of Doors, and a Council of Military Officers took upon them the Administration

Adminiſtration of the publick Affairs for ſome Days, till growing ſenſible that was a Province they knew nothing of, they put the Power into the Hands of a Pack of Knaves, under the Title of the *Committee of Safety*; their Names were, *Lambert, Desborough, Whitelock,* Sir *Harry Vane, Ludlow, Sydenham, Strickland, Berry, Lawrence, Harrington, Wareſton, Ireton, Titchburn, Braddrith, Thompſon, Hewſon, Clarke, Lilburn, Bennet,* and *Cornelius Holland.*

G E N E R A L *Monk,* who had govern'd *Scotland* under *Oliver* and *Richard Cromwell,* and then under the *Rump,* perceiving the *Engliſh* Nation under a preſent Anarchy, thought fit to exert himſelf. I will not here flatter his Memory, by aſſerting he had ſo early a Deſign of reſtoring the King; many, who were well vers'd in the Tranſactions of thoſe Times, would never allow him that Honour ; neither will I go about to diſprove thoſe who have made it their Buſineſs to applaud him. It muſt be own-ed, he was at the Beginning of the Rebellion in the King's Service ; and it is no leſs true, that he afterwards ſerv'd the Rebells ſeveral Years, being in all outward Appearance as ſtedfaſt in that Party, as the beſt of them, without ever endeavour-

Q 2

ing

ing to thwart them, whilft the two *Ufur-pers* fat on the Throne, or the *Rump* took upon them the Name of a Parliament. We will not therefore dive into his fecret Thoughts, but proceed to his Actions, in which, for a long Time, we fhall fee very little of Tendency towards a Reftoration.

As foon as the *Rump* was turned out, *Monk* declared againft thofe Proceedings of the Army; poffeffed himfelf of feveral ftrong Places, and among them, of *Ber-wick, Lambert* was then fent againft him, by the Thing call'd *A Council of State,* and Colonel *Collet* went from them to treat, whom *Monk* imprifoned, that he might not have the Opportunity of debauching his Forces. Hereupon a Project of a Free State was fet on Foot in *England,* and Commiffioners fent into *Scotland,* to con-fult with *Monk* about it. He refolved to amufe them, and fent Commiffioners to treat in *London,* who agreed with thofe appointed by the *Committee of Safety,* up-on feveral Articles; the firft of which was,

THAT the *pretended Title* of CHARLES STUART, *or any other Claiming from that Family, fhould be utterly renounced.*

Monk

MONK having other Defigns, ʋ
not ratify the Treaty; but having affen
the Nobility and Gentry of *Scotland,* w
he had before obliged by his Courtefy
mild Government, they promifed to
deavour to preferve the Peace of the
tion during his Abfence, and advanced
a Year's Tax. Whilft he was prepi
there to execute his Projects, the Peop
England, and particularly the City of
d*c*n, began to draw up Petitions for fet
fome more regular Sort of Government,
particularly for that they called a *Pa
ment,* as if any fuch could be affem
without the King's Authority. But
an Affembly they were for, which tho
Power endeavoured to obftruct, by ɪ
lifhing a Proclamation againft any fuch
titions, and ordered the pretended L
Mayor not to fuffer any to be figned.
young Fry of the City grew more boi
ous upon this Prohibition; whereupon
lonel *Hexfin* was fent into the City,
a Body of Horfe, who finding the S
fhut, and a Multitude in the Streets, k
two or three, and difperfed the reft. F
ever, the Garrifon of *Portfmouth* re
ing, and worfe Confequences being fe
the *Cabal,* which then fet at *Waling*

Q 3   H

House, voted, that a Parliament should be called in *February* next. At the same Time Forces were sent to reduce *Portsmouth*; but they were easily induced to join with those they were to have subdued, and Vice-Admiral *Lawson* declared for calling again the *Long Parliament*. After much Contention, the *Rump* was again reinstated, and began to act as imperiously as before. One of their first Actions, was, the giving of the Government of the *Tower* to that Monster Sir *Anthony Ashley Cooper*, the Idol of his Party, long after, though they joined *Weaver* and *Berners* in Commission with him. Whilst this was in Agitation, *Lambert*'s Army mostly deserted him, some going over to *Monk*, and the rest returning to their former Quarters. *Lambert* himself, thus forsaken, was sent for by the *Rump*, to curb the Forces about *London*, which began to be outragious.

THIS was the Posture of Affairs, when General *Monk* began to advance out of *Scotland*. The Gentry, in all Places he came to, making Suit to have the *Long Parliament* sit again, all whom he dismis'd with ambiguous Answers, so that none could penetrate into his Designs, and in all Probability he then had resolved no more than 'to to make his own Advantage according to Emergencies. The *Rump* dreading his Approach, refolv'd, that all Members difcharged from fitting. among them in the Years 1648 and 1649, fhould remain excluded from fitting for the future, and that Writs fhould be iffued for electing others in their Places ; none of which fo elected were to be admitted without taking the *Oath of Abjuration* of CHARLES STUART, and the whole Line of King JAMES.

U P O N this, *Monk.* hafted to *London*, and took up his Lodging in *White-Hall*, like a little Monarch, and attended the *Rump*, to whom he made a canting Speech, as the Cuftom was then, hinting at a Free-State, and defired them to take Heed of Cavaliers and Fanaticks. Then, by Order of the *Council of State* and *Rump*, he marched into the City, demanded the Affeffment they had refufed to pay, and threw down their Gates, Pofts and Chains. For this good Service he was fo well rewarded by his then Mafters, that they reduced him from a General to a Colonel, only making him one of the Seven, who were to have the Command of the Army. *Monk* thus roughly handled, thought it high Time to fecure himfelf, and accordingly having Recourfe course to his own Forces, which he brought out of *Scotland*, they resolved to stand by him, to join with the City, and to declare for a Free Parliament. This was immediately put in Execution, and a Letter to that Effect sent to the Speaker, whilst all the Bells of the City were rung for Joy, and at Night all the Streets were full of Bonfires. Next the seculed Members were summoned to meet him at *White-Hall*, whence they were conducted to the *House of Commons*, and there confirmed the Vote they had made in the Year 1648, when they had been forced thence, *That the Concessions of the late King were a sufficient Ground to proceed on for settling the Peace of the Nation.* This was in *February* 1659. Next they appointed *Monk* General of all the Forces in *England, Scotland* and *Ireland*, and having settled a Council of State to govern the three Nations, on the 16th of *March* ensuing, dissolved themselves, after having taken upon them to issue Writs for the calling of another Parliament.

WHILST the Council of State governed, *Lambert*, who had been commited to the *Tower*, making his Escape, gathered a considerable Body of the discontented Forces, which had been disbanded about *Warwick*; but

but Colonel *Ingoldsby*, sent by General *Monk*, easily routed and took him Prisoner. This settled Series of Confusions had so exhausted the People, that Oppression opening their Eyes, to perceive there could never be any Hopes of Peace or Happiness, 'till Justice were done to their much injured King. The Royalists took Heart, and ventured to appear again; the *Presbyterians*, who had been the Incendiaries, and set the Nation in a Flame, being intirely crushed by the *Independants*, thought it their safest Course to join with the *Cavaliers*, not out of any loyal Principles, (for where could any be among those who had maliciously shed so much Blood to destroy their Sovereign? but believing their former Villainies might be forgot, and themselves above those who had been all along Sufferers for Justice.

In the mean Time, *Monk* had received a Message from the King by Sir *John Greenville*, to whom he returned such mysterious Answers, as he was wont to give to others. On the 25th of *April*, 1660, that happy Year ever to be blessed by such as retain the least Spark of Loyalty, the new Parliament met, the Lords being also admitted to sit in their own House; so that something
thing

thing of the ancient Conftitution began to appear; the two Eftates, that is, the Lords Temporal and the Commons, being again in their Places, though there ftill wanted the third Eftate, being the Lords Spiritual, and the Head and Sovereign of them all, *viz.* His Sacred Majefty. Thofe two Eftates fo convened, perceiving the whole Expectation of the fo long oppreffed People, lay upon them, to find fome Expedient to deliver them from fo many Calamities, took the true and on'y method for fecuring the Peace and Felicity of thefe Kingdoms, by reftoring of the King; and accordingly on the 8th of *May,* CHARLES the Second was proclamed King of *England, Scotland, France* and *Ireland.* The true and fincere Joy of the conftant Loyalifts, who had for fo many Years lived in a worfe than *Egyptian* Thraldom, is not to be expreffed; they had fufficient Reafon to Rejoice, who had fuffered fo much for their Sovereign, and been the Object of the Malice and Contempt of all ufurping Powers, whofe chief Care it had always been to opprefs and keep them under. The old *Rebels,* who had miffed their Aim, having been themfelves crufhed, when they had hunted their King down, by another treacherous

Crew

Crew like themselves, ftruck in with the tru y loyal Party, and would be thought to exu:t in the bringing home of their King; whereas, in reality, it was to fee the Down-fall of their late Task-Mafters, who had handled them as roughly as if they had never been the Beginners and Carriers on of the Rebellion. The Multitude which for fo many Years had cry'd out, *Crucify Him*, now join'd in *Hofanna's*.

Thus all feem'd unanimous in bringing home their *David*. His Majefty in the mean Time, fends to the Parliament, the Lord *Mordaunt* and Sir *John Greenville*, with a Promife of Pardon to all Perfons in general, except fuch as the Parliament fhould think fit to be excepted; referred the Purchafers of Crown and Church Lands to the faid Parliament, and gave the Soldiers Affurances of their Arrears, and future Encouragement. The King s Letters and Declaration having been read, fix Commiffi-oners were named by the Lords, and twelve by the Commons, to go over to *Breda*, to return his Majefty their humble Thanks, and intreat his fpeedy coming over, to take up-on him the Adminiftration of the Govern-ment.

In

IN the mean Time all Things were difpofed for his Majefty's Reception, and the
Fleet fent over under the Command of General *Montague.* The King embarked on
Wednefday the 23d of *May*, againft the
Nafeby, whofe Name he altered, calling it
the *Charles*, and with a fair Gale foon arrived within two Leagues of *Dover.* There
he landed *Friday* the 25th, being met on
the Shore by General *Monk*, with whom,
and the Dukes of *York* and *Gloucefter*, his
two Royal Brothers, he proceeded by
Coach to *Dover.* After a fhort Stay there,
his Majefty was conducted by the General,
with a Guard of Horfe, and great Numbers
of Nobility and Gentry, befides an infinite
Multitude of the meaner Sort, to *Canterbury*, and there received and entertained by
the Mayor and other Magiftrates in their
Formalities, who prefented him with a rich
Bible, and a Gold Cup full of broad Pieces,
as an Acknowledgment of their Duty. The
King continued at *Canterbury* all *Saturday*
and *Sunday*, the 26th and 27th, with all
his Retinue; and on *Monday* the 28th went
on, firft to *Cobham-Hall*, a Houfe belonging to the Duke of *Richmond*, in *Kent*, and
then to *Rochefter.* On *Tuefday* the 29th,
that glorious Day, ever to be thankfully
remembred,

remembred, he set out for *London*, the number of Nobility and Gentry about him still increasing, and several Regiments of the best Horse making a Guard for him, whilst the innumerable Crowds of the common Sort strew'd all the Roads with Herbs and Flowers, and hung the Trees and Hedges with Garlands. He made a short Stay at *Black-Heath*, to view the Army, drawn up there, and about one o'Clock came to St. *George's-Fields*, where the Lord-Mayor and Aldermen waited in a Tent to receive him. *Allen*, then Lord-Mayor, delivered his Majesty the City Sword, and received it again with the Honour of Knighthood. A splendid Entertainment was there provided, of which the King took Part, and then the solemn Calvacade was continued. From the Bridge to *Temple-Bar* the Streets were railed on the one Side with distinct Standings for the several Liveries, and the other lined by the Train'd-Bands, and Gentlemen Voluntiers, all in white Doublets, under the Sir *John Stawell*. The Manner of this Triumphal Procession was as follows :

FIRST marched a Troop of Gentlemen, all in Silver Doublets, with drawn Swords, being in Number about three hundred, be-

R   sides

sides their Servants, and led by Major-General *Brown*.

ANOTHER Troop of about an hundred, in Velvet Coats, their Footmen in Purple Liveries.

A Troop under Sir *John Robinson*, with Buff Coats, Cloth of Silver Sleeves, and green Scarfs.

A Troop of about two hundred, in blue Coats laced with Silver, their Standard fring'd with Silver.

ANOTHER Troop with six Trumpets, their Standard Pike fring'd with Silver, their Footmen in Liveries of Sea Green, lac'd with Silver.

ANOTHER Troop of above two hundred and twenty, their Standard Sky, fringed with Silver, with four Trumpets and thirty Footmen, the Troop under the Earl of *Northampton*.

ANOTHER Troop of an hundred and five, in grey Coats, led by the Lord *Garing*, with six Trumpets, and their Standard Sky, with Silver Fringes.

ANOTHER Troop of seventy.

ANOTHER Troop of about three hundred Noblemen and Gentlemen, under the Lord *Cleveland*.

ANO-

ANOTHER Troop of about an hundred, their Standard black.

ANOTHER Troop of three hundred, led by the Lord *Mordant*. All these Troops finely mounted, and richly accoutered.

NEXT followed two Trumpets, with his Majesty's Arms.

THE Sheriffs Men, seventy-two in Number, in red Cloaks lac'd with Silver, and carrying Half-Pikes.

A Troop of divers Persons out of the several Companies of *London*, all in Velvet Coats, with Gold Chains, each Parcel having their respective Streamers and Footmen, with different Liveries.

TWELVE Ministers on Horseback.

HIS Majesty's Life-Guard, led by Sir *Gilbert Gerrard*, and Major *Roscarrock*.

THE City-Marshal with eight Footmen, and the City-Waits and Officers.

THE two Sheriffs, with all the Aldermen of *London*, in their Scarlet Gowns and rich Trappings, their Footmen in red Coats laced with Silver, and Waistcoats of Cloth of Gold.

THE Maces and Heralds in their rich Coats.

THE Lord-Mayor bare, carrying the Sword.

THE

THE Duke of *Buckingham* and General *Monk*, both bare.

THEN the King between his two Brothers, the Dukes of *Tork* and *Gloucefter*.

NEXT a Troop bare, with white Colours.

THE General's Life-Guard.

ANOTHER Troop of Gentry.

Laftly, Five Regiments of Horfe, with Back, Breaft, and Head-Pieces.

THE Calvacade was clofed by a vaft Number of Gentry and others, on Horfeback, richly clad and accoutered; the whole Number of it amounting to above twenty thoufand Horfe. The Streets all the Way from *Southwark* to *Whitehall*, were hung with Tapiftry and rich Silks.

IN this Manner his Majefty was conducted to *Whitehall*, where both Houfes of Parliament waited upon him in the *Banqueting-Houfe*, where he was congratulated in their Names, by the Earl of *Manchefter* for the *Houfe of Lords*, and Sir *Harbottle Grimfton* for the *Commons*. That Night was entirely devoted to Joy in all Parts, the Conduits in the City running Wine, and the Streets being made as light as Day with the Number of Bonfires.

HAVING thus brought his Majefty home with fuch univerfal Appearance of Satisfaction,

tion, there remains nothing to add to that most auſpicious Day, and the undeſerved Bleſſing then beſtow'd on an ungrateful Generation. It is true, the Parliament in that zealous Fit, with good Reaſon, eſtabliſhed a perpetual Anniverſary to be obſerv'd on the 29th of *May*, which had not only reſtor'd the King to his Right, but theſe three Nations to a State of Bliſs, had they known how to value and preſerve it; but that was not their Fate, Fanatick Rage was covered over for a while, but not quenched. The old Spirit of Rebellion ſoon broke the ſlight Fetters, which had confined it, and actuated even thoſe Wretches whom the King had loaded with undeſerved Honours and Preferments for their pretended Loyalty, after they had been ſo many Years exerciſing their Malice openly againſt the Royal Family. Mercy and Goodneſs degenerate into Vice, when they exceed their proper Bounds; the greateſt Fault in that good King, (for what Mortal is free from Frailties) was the perferring his known Enemies, who fawn'd upon him when they could do him no more Harm, and the ſlighting of thoſe who had ſacrificed their all in performing their Duty to his Royal Father and himſelf. The Court ſwarm'd with none

so much as those, who had been the chief
Instruments in bringing King CHARLES the
First to an End so shameful to the Nation;
the *Rebel-Generals*, the first *Ringleaders* of
the Multitude to Mutiny, and the very
Rumpers, who had gone through the whole
Course of Villainy, appear'd glittering in
the highest Posts, and looking down with
Scorn on those heroick Sufferers whom Loyalty had reduced to Want and Beggery. His
Majesty was soon made sensible of the Er-
ror he had been led into, by the Malice and
Avarice of those who being intent upon ag-
grandizing their own Families, regarded not
his Interest, but made all Preferments venal,
and did not stick to share among themselves
even those Estates which the *Usurpers* had
taken from such as had been their Enemies,
and the King's sincere Friends. Thus was
his Majesty put into the Hands of those who
were for making of him a glorious Prince,
in the same Manner as they had done his
Father; and indeed he was by Degrees
brought to the Brink of Ruin. The Fanaticks never ceased practising against him,
from his first being settled on the Throne,
'till it pleased God to rescue him, in his own
Time, from their bloody Designs. They
began early to disturb his Reign, and his
Mercy

Mercy encouraged them still to grown more infolent. What Affronts were not offered him by Lords and Commons? What greater Efcape could he have, after his former, before the Reftoration, than that he had at *Oxford*, from the bloody Defigns there laid againft him? Unlefs it were that of the *Rye-Houfe*, fo clofe carry'd, and fo near the Execution, for deftroying at one Stroke all the Royal Family, had not Providence, in a miraculous Manner, prevented and detected it. The *Oxford* and the *Rye-Houfe* Efcapes, may be reckoned Second and Third Reftorations, that facred Life was wonderfully both Times preferved, which reftored Happinefs to thefe Kingdoms, whilft it lafted; but it was too great a Blefling to be of long Continuance, and it was decreed, that a perverfe People fhould fuffer for their Ingratitude.

A further Defcription of the feveral Forms of Government, which by Turns prevailed, during the Grand Ufurpation.

NO fooner had we rejected that *excellent Prince*, who only had *Right*, by all
Laws

Laws Human and Divine, *to reign over us*, but prefently many of our Fellow Subjects took upon to be our Princes, and to govern us arbitrarily at their own Pleafure, in order to their own avaritious and ambitious Ends. And that firft in an *Ariftocratical* Way, as a *Senate* or *Council of State*, wherein nothing could be done without Confent of fome of the *Nobility* and *Gentry*. But it was not long (after *Royalty* was gone) but *Nobility* followed, and was excluded alfo. And *then* came *Democracy*, or the Government of the common People by their own Reprefentatives only ; which encreafed the Number of our Princes, and the Vilenefs of our Slavery by the Meannefs of our Mafters. But thefe, their own *Mercenaries*, did quickly deprive them of the Power they had ufurped and abufed ; and then came in *Stratocracy*, or the Government by the Sword, and thereby we had as *many Princes* as there were *Bafhaws* or *Major-Generals*, who perhaps, if they had out-lived their great *Sultan*, would have *canton'd* the Kingdom, and erected their feveral Provinces into fo many feveral Principalities. But by this very Means the very *Name* of Liberty and Property, which were before pretended, were quite taken away. Only there was
Liberty;

Liberty enough, and too much, indeed a lawlefs, bound efs *Licence* in Matter of *Religion*; all Ways of worfhipping God being allowed, but the true one; and all admitted to the facred Function, but fuch as were *lawfully called* unto it.; in the mean time every Sect had its *Head*, and every one that was *Head* of a *Sect*, was *Prince* of a Party; fo that we have *feen* what it is to have *many Princes*, nay, we have *felt* it to be a fore Judgment by the terrible Effects of it; which did fpread themfelves over the Face, and through the Veins, and into the Bowels of the three Kingdoms; at once embracing, involving, and confounding all Places, Perfons, and all Conditions, publick and private, high and low, facred and prophane; for from the King in his Throne, to the Beggar in the Duft, no Thing, Place or Perfon almoft hath been without *feeling* fome or other the terrible Effects of *this Judgment.* How many have loft their Limbs, their Liberty, their Country, their Eftates, their Friends, and have been reduced to extream Poverty, both at home and abroad? How many goodly Buildings and *Churches* (the glorious Evidences and Monuments of our Anceftors Piety and Charity) have been profaned and defac'd? How
many

many poor innocent Perfons of both Sexes, all Ages, and all Conditions, have been either murdered, or banished, or imprifoned, or oppreffed with Extortion of all Kinds, and of all Degrees, without any poffibility of Help, or Hope of Remedy? Laftly, How many poor *Souls,* for which *Chrift died,* have been betrayed into *Rebellion* and *Sacriledge, Schifm* and *Herefy, Uncharitablenefs* and *Cruelty,* by the horrible *Abuse* of *Preaching, Praying, Fafting, Vowing,* and all other the facred Ordinances of God? *Bifhop* Morley's *Sermon at the Magnificent Coronation of King* CHARLES II.

WHEN a violent, victorious *Faction* and *Rebellion* had over-run all, and made Loyalty to the King, and Conformity to the Church, Crimes unpardonable, and of a Guilt not to be expiated, but at the Price of Life or Eftate; when Men were put to *fwear* away all Intereft in the next World, to fecure a very poor one in this (for they had then *Oaths* to murder Souls, as well as Sword and Piftol for the Body) nay, when the Perfecution run fo high, that that execrable Monfter *Cromwell,* made and publifhed that barbarous and heathenifh, or rather inhuman *Edict,* againft the poor fuffering Epifcopal Clergy, that *they fhould nei-*
ther

ther *Preach* nor *Pray in publick*, nor *baptize*,
nor *marry*, nor *bury*, nor *teach School*; no,
nor fo much as live in any Gentleman's Houfe,
who in meer Compaffion might be inclined
to take them in from perifhing in the
Street; that is, in other Words, that they
muft ftarve and die *ex officio*, and being
turned out of their *Churches*, take Poffeffion
only of the *Church-Yard*, as fo many Vic-
tims to the remorfless Rage of a foul, ill-
bred Tyrant, profeffing Piety, without as
much as common Humanity: I fay, when
Rage and Perfecution, Cruelty and *Crom-
well-ifm*, were at that diabolical Pitch, ty-
rannizing over every Thing that looked like
Loyalty, Confcience and Conformity, fo
that he who took not their *Engagement*
could not take any Thing elfe, tho' it were
given him, being thereby debarred from
the common Benefit of the Law, in fuing
for, or recovering of his Right in any of
their Courts of Juftice (all of them ftill following the Motion of the *High One*) yet
even then, and under that difmal State of
Things, there were many thoufands who
never bowed the Knee to *Baal Cromwell*,
Baal-Covenant, or *Baal-Engagement*. Dr.
South.

WHO

WHO that looked upon *Agathocles* handling the Clay, and making Pots under his Father, and afterwards turning Robber, could have thought that from such a Condition, he should come to be King of *Sicily?* Who that had seen *Massianello*, a poor Fisherman in a red Cap, and his Angle, could have reckoned it possible to see such a pitiful Thing, within a Week after, shining in his Cloth of Gold, and, with a Word or Nod, absolutely commanding the whole City of *Naples?* And who, that had beheld such a Bankrupt, beggarly Fellow, as *Cromwell* first entering the Parliament-House, with a Thread-bare Coat, torn Cloak, and a greasy Hat, (and perhaps neither of them paid for) could have suspected that, in the Space of so few Years, he should, by the Murder of one King, and the Banishment of another, ascend the Throne, be invested in the Royal Robes, and want nothing of the State of a King, but the changing of his Hat into a Crown. *Idem.*

F I N I S.

hand-
er hs,
bxe;
Coo-
;ij,
r Fr
o.'.c
pit-
g in
l or
iole
e:d
m-
fe,
nd
m
re
e
t
l

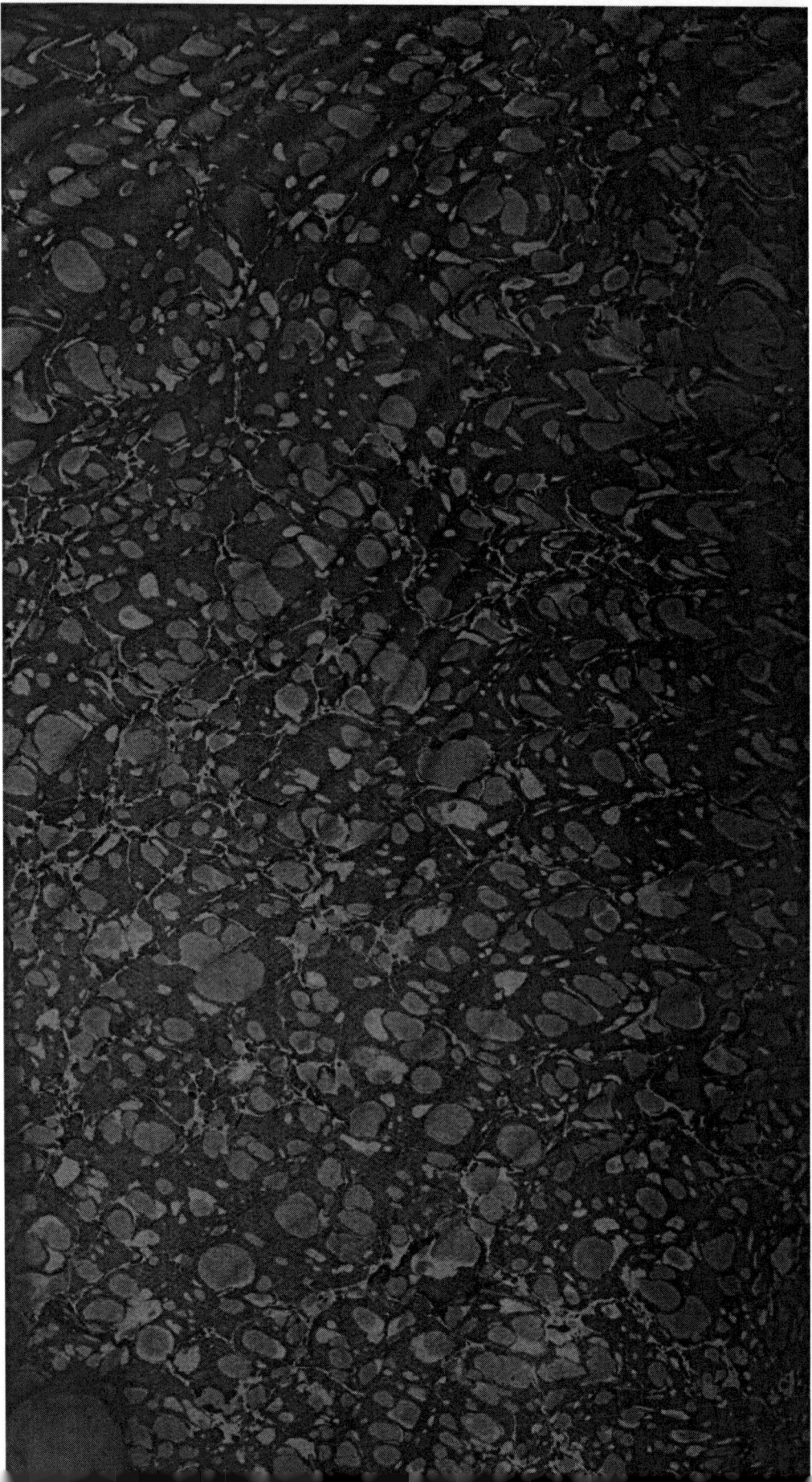

Lightning Source UK Ltd.
Milton Keynes UK
176903UK00004B/17/P

Lightning Source UK Ltd.
Milton Keynes UK
176903UK00004B/17/P